for my
next act...

for my next act...

WOMEN SCRIPTING
LIFE AFTER FIFTY

KAREN BAAR

RODALE

© 2004 by Karen Baar, M.P.H.

Printed in the United States of America
Rodale Inc. makes every effort to use acid-free ∞ , recycled paper ♻ .

Excerpt from the book *Fear of Fifty* by Erica Jong on page 23 is used with the permission of the author.

Excerpt from the film *Judy Berlin* on page 104 is used with the permission of Eric R. Mendelsohn of Caruso Mendelsohn Productions.

Results of Catalyst surveys in chapter six are used with the permission of Catalyst.

Excerpt from the essay "Can Writers Have Friends?" by Jane Smiley on pages 166–167 is used with the permission of the author.

Book design by Christina Gaugler

Library of Congress Cataloging-in-Publication Data

Baar, Karen.
    For my next act . . . : women scripting life after fifty / Karen Baar.
        p.   cm.
    Includes bibliographical references.
    ISBN 1–57954–687–0 hardcover
    1. Middle aged women.   2. Middle age.   3. Life change events.
    I. Title.
    HQ1059.4.B33   2004
    305.244'2—dc22   2003025505

Distributed to the book trade by St. Martin's Press

2   4   6   8   10   9   7   5   3   1   hardcover

Visit us on the Web at www.rodalestore.com, or call us toll-free at (800) 848-4735.

WE INSPIRE AND ENABLE PEOPLE TO IMPROVE
THEIR LIVES AND THE WORLD AROUND THEM

To Kate and Emma:

The nest may be empty, but you are always in my heart.

Love you.

ACKNOWLEDGMENTS

This book wouldn't have happened without the support and encouragement of John Collins and my intrepid agent, Angela Miller, who believed all along I had this book in me. Thanks to you both.

Gratitude and love to Pamela Hort and David Paskin for providing a much-needed refuge more times than I can count, to Sally Connolly and Semeon Tsalbins for all of those Friday night dinners and so much more, and to Carol Ripple and Jean Larson for their constant support, encouragement, and faith in me.

Many thanks to Joy Bush, Millie Grenough, Trish Loving, Donald Margulies, Kathi and Allen Mathes, Lynn Street, and Nancy Yedlin for being good friends, and to my cousin Susan Hand for her caring and support. A special thanks to my friends, Lorrie Bodger and Rozanne Gold who, as fellow writers, gave me sympathy and understanding when I most needed it.

Thanks to Carol Southern for her hard work. At Rodale, I've been fortunate to work with two wonderful editors: Stephanie Tade, whose unflagging enthusiasm for this book I treasure, and Jennifer Kushnier, the book's "final" editor, who gave it, and me, an enormous boost. I'm also grateful to the book's designer, Christina Gaugler. Thanks to Lynn Sette for tracking down all those articles, and to Julia Russo for her careful transcription of hours of tape.

Finally, I owe a great deal to all of the wonderful women I interviewed. Working on this book was a gift, thanks to your honesty and generosity in sharing your lives.

CONTENTS

introduction

ONE WEEK AFTER MY fiftieth birthday, my husband left me. We'd been together all of my adult life—nearly thirty years. We'd met when we were both twenty. It wasn't completely unexpected; despite months of couples therapy, he'd grown more and more distant, and a month earlier, on a birthday trip to London, he'd casually dropped the idea of a temporary separation. Sharing the couch in our therapist's office that day, he looked at me uncomfortably and said, "I need some time to be alone, and to think. I hope it's just temporary." That night, at my request, he packed and went to a friend's house.

That was hard enough. But three weeks later, I came home to a message on my answering machine that irrevocably changed my life. As I listened, a man I'd never met told me that his wife had left him, and that she and my husband had been having an affair for nearly eight months. Nauseated and faint, I staggered to the couch, overcome by the horror of this news. In that moment, my life became a gruesome cliché.

My husband's duplicity was stupefying. He'd told me about her: They'd met on a plane and become "friends." She was an interior designer, so they had frequent phone chats because she was giving us a free, long-distance "consult" while we redid our living room. I'd spoken to her once or twice. Hell, I'd even bought a sofa from her! I felt sick. Now, I had to live with a new reality. Not only had this woman been talking to him on the phone and meeting him all over the country as he traveled for work, but she also now had my lifelong partner's affection.

My humiliation was dreadful. When my husband first left, friends had asked, "Is there another woman?" Ever the naïf, I'd assured them that no, there was no one else; he just needed time to sort things out. We'd been in couples therapy to bridge the distance that had grown between us over the last few years and to rejuvenate our marriage, to which I was sure he was committed.

I was plunged into darkness, a maelstrom of panic, grief, rage, and pain. I'd lost not only my husband but also my best friend, my soul mate. Had he died, it would have been easier for me, so heartbreaking was his betrayal.

Everything about my life, which had seemed so secure, was suddenly up for grabs. I felt rudderless, as if he'd stolen my future. As we approached fifty, earning good money, with our children nearly grown, I had been looking forward to traveling and having a chance to enjoy more time together. No more. All my assumptions—that we'd watch our daughters finish college and marry, share the joys of grandchildren, retire and grow old together, and, most important, take care of each other—vanished. My trusting, unspoken contract with the universe—that things will work out—was broken.

Nor had I been deceiving myself about our relationship. Certainly, we didn't have the ideal marriage, but it had seemed pretty close. Relatives and friends, even our best friends, were utterly shocked.

Nothing in my life had prepared me for this. Here I was, a journalist and medical writer, whose articles had appeared in national magazines and who'd published two books. I had a master's degree in public health from Yale. I had raised two daughters and worked with smart, interesting people all my life. I was well "shrunk" after years of therapy. I thought I knew myself and other people pretty well. But I hadn't even guessed that my own husband was unfaithful. It all fell apart in an instant. I'd been left and lied to, and nothing else mattered.

For a while, it was all I could do to put one foot in front of the other; getting up in the morning was an act of sheer will. Yet the other demands on me didn't stop. I had a new book contract with an impossibly tight deadline. I was now a single parent and a solo homeowner. And even as I struggled with all of that, other people continued to need me. I had to comfort my stunned fourteen-year-old, as we both grappled with the newness of joint custody and being together only every other week. My relationship with my parents, never great, went into free fall. I had shrieking arguments on the phone with my mother—something I hadn't done since I was in my early twenties—as she cried about what my divorce was doing *to her*. (I later found research that confirmed that mother-daughter relationships often worsen during the daughter's divorce.) My sister's life was also falling apart. Meanwhile, my twenty-two-year-old was finishing college and moving back in with me while she tried to figure out what to do with *her* life; her dad couldn't lend a hand because she wasn't speaking to him. How could I help anyone when my own life had derailed so completely?

Getting through each day was all I could manage; I could barely think even one week ahead. When I did let my thoughts stray toward the future, I was terrified. How would I survive? I wondered. Could I hold on to sanity, be there for my daughters? Could I support myself as a single person? How would I retire? Who would take care of me? Would I end up a lonely, poor, embittered old woman? I knew a woman who had never gotten over her divorce; twenty years later, she was still angry and railing against her ex. Would I wind up like her?

To top it all off, I was perimenopausal. Awakened at 3:00 A.M. by hot flashes, and too worried to get back to sleep, how could I tell if it was stabs of anxiety from the broken shards of my married life or "simply" symptoms of menopause? I couldn't stop crying. I stopped eating and lost fifteen pounds. Never much of a drinker or drug taker, I quickly learned to hate Prozac and Celexa and to love Xanax, Ambien, and St. John's wort.

The self-help books about divorce, the experts, and the divorced women I knew told me my recovery would take five years. My therapist agreed with the time frame but saw the process as more than a recovery. It would be a re-creation, a redefining of my self, she promised. During those grim first few months, she said, in words that proved prescient, "It will be hard, but what's going to emerge is Karen." Now, I know she was right.

Since my marriage ended three years ago, the emotional turbulence, compounded by the hormonal changes of menopause, has often made me feel as if I'm going through a second adolescence. All of my relationships—with my daughters, my friends, my parents, men—have changed. I've made some new friends and dropped others. I've faced so many questions: How do I see myself? What is important to me? What do I want out of my career? How will I shape the second half of my life?

I don't have all the answers yet. But I've begun to reclaim my center, the solid core of *me*. More than ever before, I know who Karen is. And *For My Next Act . . .* is the result of my journey.

I didn't choose to go through the arduous task of rethinking my life; it was thrust on me with no warning. But I've realized over these last four years that, as a woman in my fifties, I'm not alone in facing questions about my future. We fifty-somethings have lived half of our adult lives. We're told that a baby girl born today can expect to live to nearly eighty. We have another twenty to thirty years ahead of us. Whether under duress or not, we are looking back at our life experiences, reevaluating where we are, and taking a critical look at the possible scripts for our futures. The hormones, the departing children, the successes, the failures, the unrealized dreams, the urge to fulfill undeveloped parts of ourselves are all colliding, forcing us to reckon with our lives in both promising and disturbing ways.

As fifty-somethings, we're breaking new ground, as we have all our lives. Born between 1943 and 1953, raised in the late 1940s and '50s, we came of age between 1963 and 1973, a period—need I remind you?—of tremendous political and social upheaval. During that time, JFK, Malcolm X, RFK, and Martin Luther King Jr. were assassinated. The riots at the Chicago Democratic National Convention and the conspiracy trial of the "Chicago Seven" occurred. Four students at Kent State University were shot dead by the Ohio National Guard. Hippies, yippies, bra burning, miniskirts, and drugs arrived on the scene. Many of us got involved in consciousness-raising groups and the civil rights and antiwar movements. Watergate happened and Nixon resigned.

We were the ones who grew up as the first major wave of emancipated women. In 1963, Betty Friedan published *The Feminine Mystique*, challenging us to get out there and do something, and suddenly we expected to go to work. Writer Linda Sexton put it aptly when she wrote that our generation is caught between the "feminine mystique" and the "feminist mystique."

We've questioned and rejected the traditional images and roles accepted by our mothers and generations of women before them. Because we didn't do what our mothers did, we're creating our post-fifty roles as we go along. And it hasn't been easy. Our early socialization is a voice lurking in the background, periodically popping up to make us feel we should be taken care of even as we also feel we need to take care of ourselves.

This inner voice further complicates an already tricky midlife transition. Terri Apter, Ph.D., writes in *Secret Paths*, a study of middle-aged women, "While their mothers before them were haunted by ideals of youth, beauty, and maternity, the adult woman of today has not escaped her mother's ghosts but added to them. Beauty, charm, grace, and youth are no less important today than they were in the 1950s; but, in addition, women in the 1990s are expected to be smart, successful, and powerful."

Our society marks many rites of passage: childbirth, birthdays, communions, sweet-sixteen parties, graduations, weddings, anniversaries, and retirement parties. However, with the exception of Native Americans—many of whom undertake a journey of renewal to a sacred place during middle age—our culture offers no such rituals to ground us during our fifties. To quote sociologist Pauline Bart, Ph.D.: "There is no bar mitzvah for menopause." We go through our midlife changes alone and adrift.

We fear getting older, and we approach middle age with a feeling of dread. This time in our lives is often characterized as a period of crisis and loss, including fading beauty, husbands who leave, menopause, mastectomies and other health problems, aging parents, empty nests, and age discrimination in the workplace. In addition, we live in a culture that reinforces negative views about aging. As Goldie Hawn's character in *The First Wives Club* said: "There are only three ages of women in Hollywood: babe, district attorney, and *Driving Miss Daisy*." No wonder we fear ending up sour, unattractive, lonely, ailing, and poor.

As I did the research for this book, however, I came upon a puzzling disconnect. Surprising as it may seem, *most women emerge from their fifties feeling better about themselves.* We needn't think of our fifties as a time when we are doomed to be buffeted by hormonal and interpersonal upheaval. In fact, it's quite the contrary: Women in their fifties experience higher levels of happiness and satisfaction than women at all other stages of life. Studies published from the 1970s through the present suggest that we feel stronger, more confident, and better about ourselves. We know what we want, and we're ready to go after it.

Based on my research and interviews, and on my own experience, I no longer view our fifties as a period of loss. Rather, it's a positive time, when we can rediscover, reclaim, redefine, or even recreate ourselves. Yes, we hit bumps, but most of us emerge from this time of life feeling better and more sure of ourselves than before. And we realize we have choices to make about the next act. Some women, like me, are jolted into reassessment by an outside event—a death, a divorce, or a major change at work. For others, the issues gradually unfold over a period of years. In either case, though, we ultimately come to see things differently.

During our fifties, we experience challenges to many of the assumptions that have guided our lives. When a friend develops breast cancer, we can no longer assume that we're safe, that death won't happen to us or to our loved ones. As our professional options narrow, we lose our sense of security in our career mobility; worse yet, we may be put out to pasture or actually lose our job. If our husband leaves or a parent dies, it's no longer a sure bet that we'll always have a protector.

In both men and women, researchers see an increase in what they call "interiority," or an introspection and taking stock. We restructure our view of life, paying more attention to the time we have left than to how long we have already lived. We know where we've been and what we've done; now we want to think about where we are going.

—⚬⚬⚬—

In *For My Next Act...* you will find stories from thirty-six women who are figuring out for themselves what really counts. This "sample" is by no means scientific, but the women come from all over the United States and from a variety of backgrounds. They are gay and straight, black and white, single, married, and divorced. Some have children and others don't. They are all middle-class or professional women. In these pages I've shared their experiences and my own, as well as information gleaned from mental health and other professionals doing research on today's fifty-something women.

I'm a veteran of the women's movement and the early days of women's "consciousness raising" groups. Today, I remain utterly convinced of the value of sharing our experiences and stories. I hope this book will encourage you to plunge bravely into this time of life with a promise that there is light at the end of the tunnel, even if you feel as if the tunnel has been long, dark, and tortuous. We are not alone. We all grapple with similar questions, and we can learn from each other, helping ourselves emerge from our fifties strongly centered and ready to live the rest of our lives with equanimity and strength.

Our fifties are a decade of enormous opportunity. Whether we've been the career woman, the supermom, the victim, or the perennial supporting player, now is the time for each of us to rewrite the script for the next act of our lives. Even when the rewrite is triggered by unavoidable or terrible circumstances, how we respond is a choice. Anaïs Nin wrote, "Life shrinks or expands in proportion to one's courage." I hope this book will inspire you to become the heroine of your own story.

who do i want to be for the rest of my life?

"Fifty years old. It is an impossible age in many ways. Not old. Not young. Not old, no. But oh, not young. What it is, is being in the sticky middle, setting one gigantic thing aside in order to make room for the next gigantic thing, and in between, feeling the rush of air down the unprotected back of the neck. I know that the transition is scary and full of awkwardness and pain—mental and physical. These dropping levels of hormones leave damage behind, like bad tenants on moving day who wreck the walls carrying things out. But once I get to the other side, I think I might be better than ever before. That's what I keep hearing. And when I think of it, that's what I've seen."

—Elizabeth Berg, *The Pull of the Moon*

I WAS STRANDED IN UTAH on September 11, 2001, stuck there after researching a story. Desperate to be home, I resorted to Greyhound and spent sixty dreary hours getting back to New York. Unlike most of my fellow travelers, I had no spouse to call from the rest stops. It was a long, lonesome trip. One night, around 3:00 A.M., I woke from a fitful sleep and felt like a tiny speck hurtling along in the darkness, alone in the middle of our vast country. It was a metaphor for my life. Eighteen months after my husband left me, I was still completely adrift. Yet underneath the awful terror, loneliness, and fear, I felt hope. I knew that the hurricane of my life had a still, centered eye, and that center was me. I had learned that whatever happened, I would be strong enough to cope. I'd come to see that I am a survivor.

What I had found, according to Jean Shinoda Bolen, M.D., author of *Goddesses in Older Women*, was my own "metis." Metis was a Greek goddess, the first wife of Zeus. She symbolizes the ability to grasp a situation, act wisely and skillfully, or take calculated risks, based on judgment. Finding your metis means that you can hold on to your sense of self and continue, even as you experience the setbacks and misery of change.

Most women are spared a ride on Greyhound, but we do make a journey as we travel through our fifties. It's a challenging trip, since it's often been hard for us to take ourselves and our own needs seriously. Until now, to avoid risk, conflict, isolation, or jeopardizing relationships, we may have allowed ourselves to be sidetracked from exploring and expressing what we wanted. We may not even have recognized our own needs as separate from those of our partners or children. Despite the women's movement, our sense of self-worth is still tied strongly to taking care of others. It's hard for many of us to follow our own self-interests and to act in direct pursuit of our own goals.

As we look back, many of us aren't sure the decisions we made were truly our own or if we simply fell into a way of being. What seemed like conscious choices at the time—becoming a nurse rather than a physician, marrying, or, because of the children, turning down a prestigious, much-desired job that required travel—may now look as if they were determined by external pressure, passivity, or fear.

At midlife, though, a host of issues converge, forcing us to ask ourselves, "Who do I want to be for the rest of my life?" Joan Borysenko, Ph.D., a former medical scientist and psychologist and author of *Inner Peace for Busy Women*, explains, "For lots of women, their fifties seem to be a period of 'don't know.' Women who've been working and raising a family were so full-speed-ahead they didn't have a chance to do much more than survive. It's the first time they can take a breath, say, Who am I, what do I want, where have I been all these years?"

As we comprehend the changing realities of our lives, we feel the sand shift under our feet. We may feel frightened or exhilarated. Sometimes we feel both in the space of a day, or even a half hour (or is that just the hormones?). For example, life hasn't yet settled down for Erica. Since turning fifty, she has left her marriage, moved to her own apartment, and become a writer. "So many things are happening. It's exhausting sometimes, and confusing, but yes, it's also OK. Exciting, too."

We realize that our self is the only constant, and that it's time to pay her some attention. Researchers describe this midlife passage in a variety of ways. Jungians hold that we give birth to our "male shadow," what psychoanalyst Carl Jung called "the animus," or aspects of our selves that we've buried deep inside to adapt our personalities to the demands and conditions of our social lives. (Likewise, men develop their "female" sides.) Studies do show that we become more outspoken, egocentric, and aggressive, less tolerant of nonsense and pretense, and less concerned about pleasing others in midlife.

What's more, when we approach menopause, we experience drops in estrogen and progesterone and a relative increase in male hormones: A woman's testosterone levels increase a whopping twenty-fold by the time menopause arrives. In other words, we're pumped. Perhaps this explains why we feel what Dr. Borysenko calls "a growing fierceness."

In any case, at midlife, many of us find the courage to experiment with a new self-definition. Sometimes, the process takes years as we struggle to achieve authenticity and to bring our lives more into line with our values. To do this, we need to reconnect to our deepest, inner core, which remains immutable: There's a Karen I've known since my earliest memories, and she's not going away. At the same time, we may rediscover aspects of ourselves that we put aside, add new ones, and discard old self-images and behaviors.

coming to terms

Before we can figure out who we want to be in the years ahead, we have to accept who we are now. To do that, some of us need to give up outdated or unrealistic expectations and let go of illusions about ourselves and others.

Most women our age started out with conventional ideas about our lives, including the husband and station wagon with kids and a dog in the back. "It was hard to grow up female in the 1950s and early sixties in this culture and not have a certain view of what your life was going to be, starting with the Barbie dolls and the wedding," says Marlene, who's single.

Many of us didn't aim high or anywhere at all, at least initially. Rachel, now fifty-five, got married right out of college. She says, "I thought I'd be married with kids and be taken care of. He was a nice guy and it was a way not to have to go to work or graduate school. I didn't have to support myself; I didn't have to be alone. It was majoring in marriage, you know?" Six months later, she had an affair. Needless to say, that marriage is long over. Since then, she has spent years alone, supported herself, and she never had the kids she took for granted. Today she has a thriving career in photography and is in a long-term relationship.

When I was growing up, I assumed I'd have a family, but that was as far as my aspirations went. Underneath the picture in my high school yearbook, the place for future career is a blank; when my daughters asked me what I planned to be, I was embarrassed to say I didn't even think about it. Meanwhile, my girls picture any number of different scenarios for themselves. Married with children? Hopefully. Career? Absolutely: from teacher to travel agent, from psychologist to doctor, from journalist to actress, and almost everything in between.

Our generation was pivotal. "I went off to college in 1963 in a bra and girdle and left with neither," says Stephanie, now fifty-eight. She remembers classmates' disapproval when she ran for class president in her large, urban high school because there had never been a female class president before. She went on to become a nationally known figure in environmental research and advocacy, getting her Ph.D. at age forty-seven. "Being challenged that way made us reach even higher," she says.

Indeed, many of us have accomplished more than we'd ever dreamed. "The one expectation I probably had was to get married and have children," says Noreen, the mother of two young adults. "I did that but also so much more. I never could have imagined that I'd be teaching at a university, that I'd travel as much as I do, that I would be thinking about doing the things in the future that I'm planning."

On the other hand, some women mourn the loss of their personal dreams. Elizabeth, for one, is married, with two children in college. She likes her work and has many friends. Life is good, she says. But has it been what she anticipated? "No. No. No. I had much more grandiose expectations for myself. I wanted to be an actress, I wanted to be a significant person in my community, and I'm not. I was going to have a perfect marriage; it was all going to be glorious and exciting. I lost the vision of what I wanted to be." Amanda, who just turned fifty-one, adds, "I wouldn't mind being in my middle twenties again. I didn't allow myself to do things—I was too afraid, and now I'd be more bold."

We have to accept that some things—a painful comment we made to a friend, a job we rejected, a conversation we never had, a man we turned away—can never be undone. And we may need to come to terms with disappointments. Ellie is a young-looking, high-energy woman. Never married, she is in a live-in relationship with a man. When she turned fifty, she had to face the fact that she is not going to have children. "I always thought I'd have them, but I got caught up in my work. Then, by the time I was in my late thirties and wanted to meet someone and have a child, my need seemed to frighten men away."

Acknowledging our regrets and forgiving ourselves the past clears psychological space for new interests and relationships. "In late middle age, you come to terms with all kinds of things you can't change about your life course—I'm never going to learn the cello, I'm not going to have that child—everything you can't do or undo," says Abigail Stewart, Ph.D., professor of psychology and women's studies at the University of Michigan in Ann Arbor. "Being able to come to some kind of resolution at this time really matters. People can get stuck if they're ruminators. It's more than just resigning yourself, it's a much more active coming to terms. You realize that, in the larger scheme of things, whatever it was doesn't matter much, and that it allowed you to do something else."

Noreen has had to make her peace with a decision she made years ago. "My husband and I made a deal when he was in business school that when he finished we'd go anyplace I wanted for school. But he got nervous because he had to support a family—we didn't have children yet, but we went where he got a job and I happened to get into school. I was very upset that I put myself second. I think I wouldn't be struggling to finish my doctorate now if I hadn't done that." Still, Noreen has accepted what happened because "I don't know that our relationship would have been able to stand me pushing at that moment, so I might not have had a marriage or the children I have now, and of course, they're very important to me."

Similarly, Lynette, a fifty-six-year-old single mother who grew up in Barbados, sometimes regrets that the father of her now thirty-two-year-old daughter wouldn't marry her. Still, even though her life has been hard, she's grateful. "I say, 'You know, Lord, if he had married me, I wouldn't be where I am now.' Sometimes I think I should write him a letter and say thank you."

Chances are, by now we've felt the "rush of air down the unprotected back of the neck," as novelist Elizabeth Berg put it, but even though we think about getting old, it doesn't rule our lives. Dr. Stewart was surprised when she found, in a series of studies of middle-aged, college-educated women, that they were not overly concerned about aging, even by the time the women were in their sixties. "We hear so much about aging and women feeling devalued or cast aside, but the women I studied experienced themselves as coming into their own," she says.

Once in our fifties, many of us feel more confident, as we create a new, more personal meaning of accomplishment. Now fifty-six, Diana had to rebuild her career and her sense of self after power politics toppled her from a high-status, corner-office job in advertising. "I used to be a real player; I was very competitive. Now, with my own firm, I have a professional life where I have everything I left behind but in a totally different, less testosterone-driven way. When I negotiate I am completely pleasant and soft-spoken; I want it to be a win–win deal where everyone is happy. In the end, I still have power but a different kind." There are other perks, too, she says. "I'm liberated. I don't have to wear high heels anymore."

Coming into our own also means that we want time, now, for ourselves. We're tired of coming up short after years of balancing other people's needs against our own. In a series of sociological studies of the Radcliffe class of 1969, the researchers found, in 1990, that "this group of women manages by setting work and family priorities at the expense of personal activities." Only 11 percent of the women said they had time for everything they wanted to do. The list of activities that they neglected or had insufficient time for were, in order: fitness, spending time with friends, creative activities, time with family members, volunteering, sleep, and religion. Some of the women simply wanted more time for puttering, reading, or being alone.

Yet learning to say "I want," to value the importance of our own emotional needs instead of reacting to or accommodating others, may be difficult since it's hard for us to express what we want without feeling selfish. "Unless it is productive, or work, or for the kids or family, our needs do not count," writes clinical psychologist Linda Edelstein, Ph.D.

Even without children, we are vulnerable to this problem. Of her live-in boyfriend, Rachel says, "He'll complain that I spend too much time in the darkroom or the studio, so I think, 'Do I really need to go, should I do this first, what does he want before I go there?' And it pisses me off that I feel I have to do that."

Turning fifty changes the equation. As hints of our own mortality begin to surface, we begin to make the switch from "I am theirs" to "I own myself," as psychiatrist Roger Gould, M.D., wrote in *Transformations*. No longer do we think it's selfish to ask, "When is it time for *me*?" Dr. Edelstein calls this "healthy narcissism." It doesn't mean that we abandon children, spouses, or other people who figure significantly in our lives, but we become more inner-directed and give less weight to what others think.

We may decide that now is the time when we can pursue things we had on the back burner or didn't have time for before. "I've gotten around to doing some of the things I want to do, even just small things," says Louisa, a wife and grandmother with a career. "I always wanted to play the piano, so I'm finally taking lessons, and I've also found a way to get exercise into my life. I don't want to live my life thinking I have forever. I want to make the most of my time." It's harder when we still have kids around, but even Marion, who has two adolescents, has managed to go off on weeklong yoga retreats. "Things have changed, and it just feels great."

paring down to the essentials

Not only are we starting to say "I want" but we're also learning to say "I don't want." Midlife is a time when we clean house, metaphorically speaking. Knowing our time is limited leaves us no time for nonsense. We want to eliminate the unnecessary, whether it's clothes, work, friends who don't support us, or maybe even mates. Or, as Lola puts it, "I want to get all the jerks out of my life." It becomes a lot easier to say no.

We also want to give up "having it all" because we've found that having it all means "doing it all." Says Stephanie, "We gave each other something in those days of the women's movement, saying, We can do this, we're going to challenge that. Of course, we weren't giving up all that women had traditionally done, we were just adding to it. And I think a lot of us are tired."

Some women find themselves so estranged from their husbands that they need to dissolve their marriages. Erica describes this feeling: "I knew I had to get out of that place, that apartment, that marriage—that everything—or I would not be able to survive."

Major drama isn't a necessary prerequisite to simplifying our lives. Noreen, who is reassessing some of her friendships, says, "My active goal right now is to not have every relationship be one where I take care of other people, which seems to be my pattern." Other women I interviewed also talked about ending friendships or changing the ground rules to make them less complicated. "I don't want to waste my energy; I don't want to do what I don't want to do. I've learned to say no," says Stephanie.

No aspect of our lives, except, perhaps our children, is spared the reappraisal. For most of her adult life, Ruth put in long hours volunteering for community organizations in the small Northwestern suburb where she lives. "I still tutor because I like it, but I'm doing much, much less," she says. "I'm learning to preserve time for myself in a way that I couldn't before, when I couldn't say no. It does get easier to do that in your fifties; maybe that's one of the positive things about getting older. I am very protective of my time."

finding ourselves

In the process of peeling away what's not essential, we begin to cure ourselves of what Gloria Steinem has called the "female psychological disease," of knowing what other people feel better than what we ourselves are feeling. When we do this, Steinem suggests asking what she calls the "revolutionary" question: "What do *I* think?" We'll then start to act out of our own inner values and needs, rather than conform with cultural, familial, or social expectations.

It's all so invigorating. "I feel so much more self-confident now that I'm in my fifties," says Louisa. "I don't feel like I need to try to be something I'm not. It seems I was never quite sure who I was or what defined me, but that's one of the good things about getting older. I have a sense of myself. It just took fifty years to develop."

When Erica left her marriage, she also abandoned her career as a graphic artist. "I hated it, and I decided I wasn't going to be fifty years old and still doing that. I would rather work at a bookstore if I have to. The minute you admit these kinds of feelings to yourself, you make something else happen." Now she writes nonfiction to support herself, which enables her to write fiction in her spare time. Ultimately, she hopes to make the fiction her livelihood. Meanwhile, she enjoys all of her writing far more than her previous design work. "I write out of my life, whatever is going on. I have a wonderful time; they're paying me to sit around and think, which is like heaven."

Likewise, Gloria got married when she was 19. "My mother always said, 'I never worried about you; you were married.' Well, she should have worried. I wish I had done differently; I wish I had had time for myself." But it's never too late. After a major health scare, Gloria changed her life. "It helped me figure out what's important, what I want to do, and how to go and do it." She took a year's leave of absence from her job teaching young children and became a tai chi instructor. When she returned to work, she started a tai chi program at her school. "They love it. Tai chi is a really powerful thing to do with kids."

Some of us return to things we used to do, or to goals we previously suppressed. Many of us who did have ideas about what we would like to do kept these dreams in the closet until the children were out of the house. "It's not about redefining myself; it's more a time to pursue things I put on the shelf, happily, for a time," says Lola, who's revived her love of quilting and sewing by revamping one of her children's bedrooms into her sewing room. Indeed, writes psychologist Ruthellen Josselson, Ph.D., in *Revising Herself*, "As women grow, they struggle to make space for these disused or disavowed parts of the self, widening the expanse of identity to encompass what was left behind."

Elizabeth used to be an artist, but she let it slide long ago. Today, she continues to work as a doctor, but as she goes through her fifties, she's had a resurgence of creative energy, which she's channeling into writing plays and short stories. "There are moments when I'm doing something creative and I'm in a different zone; it's very exciting. I love it, when I'm walking down the street and instead of worrying about something, I'm thinking, 'How can I move the plot there? What should this character be doing?'"

Even women in the spotlight decide to make changes. In a February 2003 article in the *New York Times* about Jane Pauley's decision to leave NBC after twenty-seven years with the network, Bill Carter reported, "At fifty-two she still found herself wondering, 'What's next, or even, what is it I really want to do?'" Ms. Pauley had been thinking about making this change since sending her twins off to college a year earlier. Besides, she said, "'I think women think a lot about cycles, biological and personal. This year another cycle came around: My contract was up. It seemed an opportunity to take a life audit.'"

A life audit. That's a good way to describe what we go through during our fifties. As time becomes more precious, we ask ourselves— or are forced to ask—major questions: Have I made mistakes that I can change? Can I improve my relationships with my husband, kids, and friends? Am I happy in this job? Am I doing what most fulfills me, or can I find a better way to spend my time? We may grow tired of pretending we're someone that we're not and look for ways to express our true selves.

To be sure, throughout our lives, we change and we stay the same. As we progress through our fifties, we reconnect with our essential selves, accepting who we've always been and, at the same time, allowing space for new parts of ourselves to grow. As the following chapters will show, some of us make peace with things as they are, and others take a deep breath and plunge into the unknown. In either case, the goal, I think, is to feel as Marsha—who left her husband, quit her job, and started a new career—puts it: "I'm living the life I want to lead. I'm definitely the author of this life."

TAKING STOCK AND MOVING FORWARD

∾ Can you remember how you envisioned your life when you were a girl? A teenager? A college student? How is it different, and how is it the same? What did you imagine yourself doing that you're not doing?

∾ Did you make the choices that have determined the course of your life? Have there been any particularly critical decisions or events that have shaped your life?

∾ Often, before we can move ahead, we need to accept what happened in the past. Are there past events in your life that you dwell on? Do you feel stuck in regret for mistakes you think you made? Perhaps a counselor could help you get over disappointments and sorrows so you can leave the past behind and move into the future.

∞ How is your health? Do you feel burned out juggling kids, career, and partner? Can you think of ways to restore yourself?

∞ Can you carve out a few hours a week just for yourself?

∞ Have career and family obligations made your social life nonexistent? How would you like it to be?

your significant other

shifting ground in a familiar landscape

> *"What was happening to me in the second part of my life? I was getting myself back and I liked that self. I was getting the humor, the intensity, the balance I had known in childhood. But I was getting it back with a dividend. Call it serenity. Call it wisdom. I knew what mattered and what did not. Love mattered. Instant orgasm did not."*
>
> —Erica Jong, *Fear of Fifty*

As women in our fifties, we know who we are. Many of us have found autonomy through our work, and we look for give-and-take and a balance of power in our relationship to our significant other in a way that we may not have done earlier. Jungian psychoanalyst James Hollis, Ph.D., in *The Middle Passage*, describes the "hidden agenda" of marriage as: "I am counting on you to make my life meaningful. I am counting on you to always be there for me. I am counting on you to read my mind and anticipate all my needs. I am counting on you to complete me, to make me a whole person." Marriages that endure are the ones where both partners have come to terms with such unrealistic expectations.

Satisfying relationships are characterized by what psychologist Judith V. Jordan, Ph.D., calls "mutuality." Two people recognize each other's needs, express their fears, worries, desires, and joys; yet they don't lose themselves as individuals and merge into a "couple." Instead, they remember that ultimately, they are emotionally responsible for themselves. "Mutual relationships in which one feels heard, seen, understood, and known, as well as listening, seeing, understanding, and emotionally available, are vitally important to most people's psychological well-being," write Dr. Jordan in a chapter in *Women's Growth in Connection*. "In many ways we come to know ourselves through relationship."

In a mutual relationship, not only do we help our partner, but we also learn about ourselves in the process. Louisa and her husband are very close, she says. "We balance each other. He was looking to get away from anyone who was like his mother and sister, and I don't think he could have picked anybody more different from them than I am. And I was looking for somebody who was emotive and passionate, and he really is that way. We fit each other's needs to begin with, and then we've just kept trying to share things and work on communicating during the course of the marriage. It's good because he makes it easier for me to understand where my deficits are, and I'm there to help him figure out what his issues are. It's good that way; it really is."

Marriages do change, often for the better, as we enter our fifties and see children off to college. Many of us are more financially secure than we've ever been. We're also secure in who we are, and this assurance offers opportunities for new closeness. Indeed, many of the women I interviewed are finding renewed love, intimacy, and shared pleasures in their marriages.

In our fifties, we often have more time to do the things we always wanted to do with our husbands or significant others. This may be delightful, but often we find that we have some work to do. Our challenge is to adjust the balance between ourselves and our partners, allowing our growing need for autonomy to flourish along with our marriages, so that we can share the journey ahead with the people we love.

The empty nest or other changes may prompt us to question our marriages or take a new look. Because of our long life spans, we spend many years with our partners, and good relationships allow room for both individuals to change and grow. As we each grow more sure of ourselves, we have the opportunity to have richer, deeper relationships.

Of course, many fifty-something women are divorced, widowed, or never married. Many of us have also chosen alternatives to marriage. Of the thirty-six women I interviewed, eighteen were married, five for the second time; eight were divorced and single; two were widowed; five were divorced and in another important relationship; and three had never married.

Between 1970 and 1998, the proportion of women ages thirty to thirty-nine who never married nearly tripled. The stereotype of a single, middle-aged woman has changed. No longer are we dismissed as unattractive "spinsters." According to the authors of *Lifeprints*, a book-length study of the lives of 300 midlife women, "If one were to draw a composite of the employed, single woman in middle adulthood today, it would be of an active woman, seriously involved with her work, who maintains close ties with her own extended family, often including nieces and nephews. She is close to friends who give her support and comfort in time of trouble." Furthermore, they say, she may or may not be involved in an intimate relationship, but the lack of a partner doesn't negate her self-esteem or satisfaction with her life.

This is particularly true when we have *chosen* to remain single. Lynette made a conscious decision not to marry. As a young woman in Barbados, she became pregnant, only to find that the baby's father wouldn't marry her. "For the longest time I did not trust men; I wore a face that told them, 'Stay away from me.' And I couldn't come to grips with the idea of a stepfather for my kid. I didn't want to ever be in a situation where I'd have to choose between my partner and my child." Lynette grew up with strong matriarchs as her role models—first her grandmother, and then her mom—so although she "wouldn't mind having a companion," she has no regrets.

On the other hand, some women, like Annie, regret not having the right person. "I would like to have a partner. I haven't given up, but it's just chance. It's hard to be a single person. Sometimes, I feel like all the world's in a couple."

Of course, it's never too late. Ellie met her current boyfriend when she was 44, and they've been living together ever since. "We'll probably get married, which is an emotional thing for me. Imagine, being a bride at fifty-two," she laughs.

There's also a growing number of couples who have chosen to live together and not tie the knot. Of the 7.6 million men and women cohabiting in the United States in 2000, 47 percent of the men and 42 percent of the women were age thirty-five or older. We reject marriage for many reasons. Rachel, once divorced, has lived with a man in what she calls a "committed relationship" for ten years. Remaining unmarried suits her because she fears marriage will somehow spoil a good relationship. She likes to feel as if she has an out. "I know it's not rational, but I need an escape hatch," she says.

Similarly, Joanne has been in a deep, stable relationship with Ted for twenty-eight years. However, having already been married and divorced, she is scornful of marriage as a legal and religious institution. "The sanctity of the state bestowing its legal status on the marriage didn't do diddly-squat for keeping my marriage alive before," she says. "Nor did getting married within a church. What keeps people together is their loving commitment to each other, to give love and be loved, to be respected, and to really enrich each other's lives. With Ted, I get great pleasure and a feeling of being loved and cared for."

Dorothy and her partner, Lucy, agree. "We're married in all but the eyes of the law," Dorothy says. "We've been together more than seventeen years and are parents of a fourteen-year-old child."

However we choose to be with our partners, relationships often change as we go through our fifties. If we've had children, their departure allows us more time and energy to focus on our spouses. "There are different phases you go through in a relationship," says Joanne. "First, you're finding out about each other, then you're so focused on bringing up the kids. Afterward, there's still an extraordinary amount of unexplored and maybe unexplained terrain about who and what you are and what your relationship is. To think that there are still things we don't know, that there's more we can find out about ourselves and each other—it's exciting!"

We want to share interests and emotional connectedness with our partners. "I see myself as an independent person. I have my own career. I could support myself if I had to," says Noreen, a college teacher. "But Frank cares what kind of day I had, and that gives meaning to it all." Sarah couldn't find the words to describe her marriage. "It's like asking what do you get from being alive." What's helped her thirty-two-year-old marriage thrive is "determination, love, and luck," she says. "And, in particular, figuring out our boundaries, especially between work and private life."

changing roles

If both partners are going through midlife changes, however, this can be a turbulent time for us. Moreover, men and women often move in different directions as they age, and that alters the balance of power in a relationship.

Also, if we've tended to defer to our mates in the past, we may arrive at a better understanding of our own strengths. As sociologist Pauline Bart, Ph.D., put it in "The Paradox of the Happy Marriage," "There are few traumas greater than . . . the wife's discovery of her husband's dependencies; than the discovery of her own gut-superiority in a thousand hidden crannies of the relationship; than the realization that in many situations his judgment is no better than hers; that he does not really know more than she; that he is not the calm, rational nonemotional dealer in facts and relevant arguments; that he is, in brief, not at all the kind of person the male stereotype pictures him to be. Equally, if not more, serious is her recognition that she is not really the weaker vessel, that she is often called upon to be the strong one in the relationship."

Some researchers have written of a reversal in sex roles during midlife. According to this theory, women tend to gain strength as we age, becoming more self-assertive and less dependent on our partners. Meanwhile, men become needier and, especially as they approach and go through retirement, may become more invested in the relationship.

There are many possible explanations for these changes. According to psychoanalyst Carl Jung, middle-aged men and women begin to explore their "shadow" selves, or aspects of our personalities that we denied or repressed before. Women, then, become more "male" and men become more "female." Others suggest that the changes women experience have to do with biochemistry, in particular a shift in the ratio of male to female hormones.

Even though we may be more male, we're still doing "women's work." Women still bear primary responsibility for hearth, home, and family. After years of serving the emotional needs of others, we may see this as our time, finally, to find our own self-expression. Describing the subjects in one of her many studies of middle-aged people, social psychologist Bernice Neugarten, Ph.D., wrote in "The Awareness of Middle Age," "Most of the women interviewed feel that the most conspicuous characteristic of middle age is the sense of increased freedom. . . . Whether married or single, the typical theme is that middle age marks the beginning of a period in which latent talents and capacities can be put to use in new directions."

We become aware of an opening, and we can't wait to explore and take on new challenges. We're excited by all of our prospects. Sarah and her husband had organized their lives—where and how they lived—around his career. They had a traditional marriage; she stayed at home or worked part-time to raise their four children, while his career got "full space and possibility." Now, it's her time, says Sarah. "It's a real turning point for me. I have lots of energy, and I feel like I'm in some kind of gestation period—I don't know yet where my energy will take me."

Sarah says it's different for her husband. "He's had this wonderful job, and now he's wondering, does he really want to do it for twenty more years?" Just as we're feeling expansive, our partners' lives may begin contracting. Betty Carter, renowned family therapist and author of *Love, Honor and Negotiate*, puts it this way: "The man is now thinking of taking off an extra day for golf, spending more time to-gether, cutting back at work, or retiring. She is thinking, 'Hot diggity dog, at last I have my career.'"

If retirement is on the horizon for either us or our husbands, the adjustment can be tough. In a 2001 study on couples' transitions into retirement, Cornell University sociologist Phyllis Moen, Ph.D., found that marital strife was highest when men retired first, probably because they weren't used to being alone at home, and because both partners were uncomfortable as their roles, status, and power in the marriage changed. Part of the problem is that, despite our being "liberated" women, we have still done more, if not most, of the cooking, cleaning, laundry, and shopping. Ms. Carter says, "Men have not said, 'Watch me take over the household.' There's lots of 'new man' talk, but the new man still goes to the supermarket with a list his wife has written."

Once men retire, they may become more needy. Women tend to have ongoing friendships that meet our emotional needs. In contrast, many men reveal their inner lives only to their wives, and if their other relationships have centered on the workplace, they may be facing isolation.

Besides, having focused so intensely on their careers, men may not know how to occupy themselves as work begins to wind down. Until now, Noreen's husband filled his time with his job and his children. "He only knows fast-forward and dead stop. He is a black-and-white person and doesn't know shades of gray. He's having to learn what to do with his leisure time now that the kids aren't there, and he's kind of lost." It's different for Noreen; although she holds down a full-time job, she also has a reading group, a yoga class, and many friends.

Sue, a nurse-midwife, wonders if her workaholic husband will ever retire. "It's sad that he doesn't have any interests; he'll probably just keep working. Thank heavens I've got my own life." On the other hand, some women enjoy a new closeness with their husbands. Louisa says, "We are each other's best friend. We spend more time with each other than we do with anybody else."

As we get older, our other interests grow in value. In a paper presenting the results of eight different studies of middle-aged or older couples in Israel, Ariella Friedman, Ph.D., wrote that women were happier in their marriages when they were free of the stress of kids at home. They had developed new interests or renewed old ones, had more social activities, and did more volunteer work. Meanwhile, the men rarely developed new interests and were dependent on their wives for their social lives.

Since women don't usually identify with their work to the extent that men do, we may have a significant advantage. Louisa's husband, for example, faces a major shift as he ages because his job as a carpenter is so physical. "I think he's struggling with getting older more than I am. His self-image is very tied up in his work and it's hard for him to imagine himself doing anything else, or having other interests."

At least retirement is planned. During lean economic times, couples may have to cope with the economic and personal consequences of unexpected layoffs. One colleague told me that her husband had been laid off after more than twenty years at a publishing house. "It's grim. And it's not just the lost income, but also the loss of purpose and identity. He's so depressed."

In many cases, then, while men may face a sense of personal diminishment, women have a growing sense of personal power and confidence. It's important for us to be aware of our partners' feelings and use our own newfound strengths to help them adjust.

what does (or doesn't)
go on in the bedroom

Sometimes, we play out in the bedroom the changes we're experiencing in other areas of our lives. For example, as we become more assertive, we may want to act more on our own sexual feelings, rather than deferring our pleasure to our partners' needs. "If I'm not in the mood," says Joanne, "I'm no longer willing to do it just to keep Ted cheery. On the other hand, I'm more aware of and honest about my sexual feelings and, as a result, our sex life is deeper and more satisfying for both of us."

For many women, sex in midlife becomes much more gratifying than it has ever been. According to sex researchers William H. Masters and Virginia E. Johnson, "There is no reason why the milestone of the menopause should be expected to blunt the human female's sexual capacity, performance, or drive." In addition, our new (and wonderful) freedom from the fear of getting pregnant sometimes unleashes new sexual energy.

We also may appreciate sex more since, just as we're becoming more interested, our partners may be experiencing a decline in sexual desire and want to make love less often. Still, for many women, explains Lillian B. Rubin, Ph.D., in *Women of a Certain Age*, "the waning of the intensity and frequency of their husband's sexual need brings an important new dimension to their own sexual experience. Until this happens, many women never have the chance to feel the full force of their own sexual rhythm, never get to experience the frequency or potency of their own sexual desires."

As always, sex is complicated. At this point in life, both men and women may have lowered libido as well as physical changes that can take a toll in the bedroom. A growing number of men have occasional or frequent problems with impotence. For us, vaginal dryness or other symptoms caused by dropping levels of estrogen (conditions easily remedied) may make intercourse uncomfortable or undesirable.

And let's remember that, as Dr. Christiane Northrup wrote in *The Wisdom of Menopause*, "the brain is the biggest sex organ in the body." Women who are feeling unattractive or inadequate usually have less interest in sex; the better we feel about ourselves, the more likely we are to enjoy sexual experiences. Even more significant, sexual boredom usually masks something more. Simmering resentments or old conflicts with our partners about other issues all too often stifle passion and the ability to achieve orgasm.

Inequality in the bedroom can also be a problem. Psychologist Irene P. Stiver, Ph.D., described a familiar scenario in a chapter in *Women's Growth in Connection*, in which she wrote, "For many men, one of the few settings in which they can give expression to their needs to be given to and cared for and can experience deep feelings, and still feel manly, is in the bedroom. There the man can be at his macho and phallic best while also allowing himself to be entitled to gratification of his needs for closeness and connection." Yet, women may not respond. "As long as the woman feels her needs are not being met, she will, unconsciously at least, be resentful and hostile toward any expression of the man's neediness."

Sadly, many of us discover just how repressed we were—and how much we were missing—only in retrospect, when, as divorcees or widows, we discover new sexual excitement and pleasure. Indeed, results from the Melbourne Women's Midlife Health Project, a large, long-term study in Australia, demonstrated that middle-aged women who had a new partner often reported an increase in sexual desire, enjoyment, and arousal.

On the other hand, we may enjoy deepening emotional intimacy with long-term partners. As Dr. Rubin writes in *Women of a Certain Age*, "The years of sharing the same bed means they know each other better, are more likely to know what will bring sexual pleasure, are more trusting, and, therefore, more able to be interdependent." In addition, couples who've been together a long time have an easier time adapting to physical changes, whether that means altering patterns to focus less on intercourse or accommodating a partner's disability.

are we up for the challenge?

Here's the midlife marriage paradox: Even if we are growing in separate ways—women reaching out and men turning inward—our relationships with each other may actually improve.

The reason? Instead of a collision course, we may actually get lucky and cross paths, arriving at a place where we each value the relationship equally. In the Israeli studies by Dr. Friedman, she and other researchers found that when men grew older, they ranked marriage and family as much more important than they did when they were young. As the men began to more highly appreciate their marriages, they came to share common ground with their wives, for whom marriage and family had been key all along.

Now, because our partners see our relationships as more central, we have a real opportunity to communicate better and enjoy our marriages more. As the demands of child rearing and career begin to wind down, we develop new structures for our lives. "In terms of how much time we spend together, I think we have a balance that suits us now," says Lola. "We eat dinner together every night and spend the weekends together. In the evenings, he goes into his study or to the gym, and I go into the family room or upstairs. We also have our little rituals. For instance, we commute together to work and we watch a movie every Friday night."

Arriving at a balance between the time we spend together and apart makes a big difference in our enjoyment of each other. Often, we find we have separate interests and pursuits. Many of us come to accept that our partner doesn't share a particular passion with us, so we pursue it alone. "There's that whole thing about blaming your partner for all the things you aren't," says Joanne. "You know, we say, 'I'm not emotionally or intellectually fulfilled because he's not that kind of person,' or 'I'm not politically active because he's not.' I've decided that that's a ten-year-old's attitude."

This also means respecting your partner's passions. Joanne is untroubled by the many hours Ted spends listening to sports; likewise, he acknowledges her desire to do volunteer work in her church. Similarly, Elizabeth makes sure her husband has time to putter with his antiques while she is free to go to the theater and art galleries with her friends.

When the house quiets down, the transition isn't always smooth. We may be lucky and remember what we liked about each other, so we easily renew the relationship. On the other hand, we may find that raising a family masked a growing lack of interest as well as differences in style, goals, and dreams that are too much to live with now. After my husband left and I had time to look back on the causes, I realized that we had a basic difference that had been obscured by the hubbub of daily life. I've always been someone who needs time to myself, while he cannot be alone. Of course we had other issues—a lack of shared interests, different friends—that helped to break up the marriage, but our discrepant needs for solitude was one of the more important ones.

As we get older, declining physical stamina may force us to change how we spend time together. "One of the things that has been sustaining in our relationship is that we enjoy doing physical things together—skiing, canoeing, biking, walking, hiking," says Joanne. "But our ability to do those things is lessening, and I'm wondering how not doing them is going to affect our relationship. Already, Ted has had to give up skiing because his knees are bothering him."

Ruth, on the other hand, worries about the future in a very immediate way as she and her husband cope with her inevitable decline from her Parkinson's disease. "He doesn't have the patience and the constitution to avoid becoming frustrated and angry. As I get worse, I'm afraid of what that will do to him. He has trouble hearing me sometimes. It's partly because my voice is a little softer, but it's also because he is hard of hearing and he won't get a hearing aid. It angers him when he can't hear me. Then, I think when I can't walk straight or fast enough, that also will anger him, and I'm not sure how he will come to terms with this. It's a big challenge I face in the next fifteen years."

Dealing with declining health and other weighty concerns requires flexibility, patience, forgiveness, and tolerance. These are the hallmarks of a strong long-term relationship—says Sarah Eldrich, a family attorney in New Haven, Connecticut, who has handled divorce cases for many years and, incidentally, has been married for more than twenty-five years herself. "You're going to have moments when you can't stand it for another minute. You have to see things in yourself you don't want to see, and you may have to accept things about your spouse that you don't like. When it's bad, you have to figure out how to make it better and do it. It's incredibly hard work."

One of the toughest pieces is handling each other's temperaments. Hopefully, if we've been together a while, we've learned a thing or two. Says Ruth of her husband, "He has a tendency to develop these moods where he really withdraws emotional support. That used to be horribly damaging to me, and it still hurts when it happens. But over time, I've learned to cope with it better and it affects me less."

Sorting out whose emotional issues are whose can be a challenge. Says Ms. Eldrich, "So many people are not prepared to deal with an unhappy spouse, and there are going to be numerous times throughout a marriage when one spouse or the other is unhappy. Too often, what happens is the partner thinks it has to do with them and takes it personally, when it's really a question of the unhappy partner struggling with his or her own issues."

Even mundane considerations, like how we divvy up household chores, can have deeper repercussions. Switching who paid the bills, for example, had surprising results for Amanda and Steve. What had seemed like merely stylistic differences actually had emotional impact. "He used to do the checkbook, but he did a terrible job," she says. "We would get dunning notices, people calling us. To some extent, because he grew up with no money, it didn't bother him. For me, it was humiliating. On the other hand, he's not a spender. Since we switched, it's a lot better. I don't like to get the phone calls, so I pay the bills more promptly. But I'm also the person who needs to look at the MasterCard bill and say, 'Holy shit, I charged that much?' When I mess up, I always have guilt, guilt, guilt, shame, guilt, shame about this or that. Since he's more lax, he's also much more forgiving, and that's been good for me."

By now, successful couples have also developed ways to negotiate the "outside" world together. For lesbian or interracial couples, this may be a particular challenge. When Dorothy and her partner bought an apartment in New York City, they had to appear before the building's co-op board to be approved. Dorothy explains their strategy:

"We didn't stay in the closet, but we have always found if we both get into a 'femme' mode, people respond better. So, we wore flowered dresses and acted like responsible professional women. Besides, we were raising a child. Sure enough, one of the old ladies said, 'They're such nice girls; it's too bad they don't make enough money to each have their own apartment.' Everybody else on the committee got it. We had no problem." Similarly, Amanda and her husband, who is African-American, chose to remain in the city, rather than move with their children to a mostly white suburb. "We've made conscious choices that would reduce the risk of our children being hurt or angered."

Whatever the issues, long-term relationships require good communication. When children move out, the silence can be deafening. We may need to learn how to talk to each other again. Or we may have to figure out when not to talk, or how to achieve companionable silence.

Sometimes, we realize that certain kinds of conversations are just not going to happen. Joanne explains, "I wish he would push us to engage at a much deeper level than we do, but he's not a person who wants to talk about his emotions or what he's experiencing. He won't discuss different facets of our relationship, what we think about things, our perceptions of the world, or what we're reading. Maybe it's a male thing, maybe it's him, or maybe it's what we've fallen into."

In comparison, Laura and Michael are lucky to talk to each other at all. Together for seventeen years, they've found that raising their adopted toddler has pushed their relationship to the limit. "In the beginning of our relationship we fought a lot," she admits. "Then we worked stuff out, more or less. Now we're having to do it all over again. We're starting to see what our strengths are as a couple, and that we can negotiate the pitfalls. We have to be respectful of each other, even when we're in the midst of it."

Respect is a biggie. So is affection. According to psychiatrist Harvey L. Ruben, M.D., in *Supermarriage*, happily married couples don't take love for granted; they still treat each other as if "courting." Rona Ahrens, a psychotherapist in private practice, says, "Simple things are so important. Men and women lose the ability to fight clean. Instead, they get aggressive, or passive-aggressive, or go Dolly Doormat. It's important to be polite. Send flowers; give your spouse a kiss hello or good-bye. Be able to say, 'I need fifteen minutes to myself,' rather than just locking yourself away."

Also, each of us has to own up to the part we play in the relationship. Maria Tupper, a clinical social worker in private practice, explains: "People say, 'Everything between us would be okay if only you would . . .' I have them list as many of those things as they can think of, and then take the list and see how many apply to themselves. Sometimes it helps them take more responsibility for their own role."

not sweating the small stuff

For most of us, maturity brings tolerance, and we make compromises and concessions we never expected to make. Sometimes, staying together is merely a matter of deciding it's okay to put up with minor distractions. As we get older, we also, hopefully, get wiser. Because we see our lives from a broader perspective, we spend less time worrying about the little things. So what if he chews with his mouth open or he doesn't squeeze the toothpaste tube from the bottom? There are more important things in life.

However, accepting life with a misshapen tube of toothpaste is different from resigning yourself to major problems, such as alcoholism, drug addiction, and philandering. Sometimes we're not willing to let our needs for emotional intimacy go unmet any longer, or we realize that the man we married has problems that make a relationship impossible. If the issues are serious enough, we may have to leave.

Even today, though, with so many of us able to support ourselves, many women stay in troubled relationships because it's too scary or complicated to think about the alternative. Elizabeth, who has thought about leaving her husband numerous times over their thirty years together, says, "I stayed in a difficult marriage. Certainly it had something to do with feeling responsible for him. But I also did it because it was too hard to think about leaving. There's nothing pure—it's not like I was purely generous, nor was I purely selfish. I was scared of change."

And perhaps she fears loneliness. In one of John Updike's stories, a long-married woman, after enumerating what she doesn't like about her husband, says, ". . . but I've never been lonely with you. I've never for an instant felt alone when you were in the room."

If we can't consider leaving the marriage, we may go through a period of adjustment in order to change what we can or accept what we cannot alter. In many cases, the pros far outweigh the cons in a long-term relationship. "I realize I'm never going to be satisfied with the way Jim relates to our kids. But now that they're out of the house, it's not so big an issue, and it's not worth jeopardizing an otherwise very good marriage," says Lola.

Some of us learn how to work around the issue. Joanne is sometimes driven to distraction by her partner's indecisiveness. "A lot of our decisions are made by not deciding, out of inertia. Should we roof the house, go to an event, buy something? Things don't happen because of his unwillingness to decide. If it's something I can do without him, I will. Otherwise, I've learned to manipulate things to get my way more often."

Likewise, Sue has reconciled herself to her husband's workaholic habits. She'd like to travel, but she knows it's not going to happen with him. Instead, she looks to other people. For instance, she just went to Central America with an old friend to celebrate her fiftieth birthday. "I wish he didn't work so hard, so we would do more together. But after you've been married almost thirty years you realize there are some things that are never going to change, and that's one of them."

Counseling is a valuable option. "We use therapy, either separately or together, the way other people use doctors," says Noreen. "When we come to an impasse and we don't know what to do if one or the other of us is unhappy, we go talk to the therapist, and that's helped a lot."

And even though she's been unhappy at times, when I asked Elizabeth what she gets from her marriage, she replied, "I get stability, a safety net. No matter where I am, I'm connected. Like a helium balloon, he brings me to earth. It's a nice thing; it's a part of my life I don't have to think about. And he's the one I come home to at night."

Long-term marriages offer us something else, too. Despite (or maybe because of) her experience working with divorcing couples, Ms. Eldrich thinks it's worth staying in for the long haul. "I still believe marriage is incredible, if you can find a way. Sharing your life with someone over the years is better than having multiple relationships with different people. When I talk to people who get divorced when they're older, their greatest difficulty is that when they find someone else, that person has none of the history." Shared history creates bonds that are irreplaceable and helps couples weather the storms.

marriage: good for our health?

We certainly reap a host of benefits—companionship, financial security, someone to grow old with, sexual and emotional intimacy, the feeling of being loved and cared for—when we stay happily married. According to Shelley E. Taylor, Ph.D., professor of psychology at UCLA, in *The Tending Instinct*, "For decades, psychological studies have found that marriage—not money, not children, not a host of other things that could make you happy—is the primary determinant of emotional well-being." (Interestingly, cohabitation doesn't necessarily provide the same psychological protection as marriage, although researchers aren't sure why.)

In addition, married people of both sexes have lower rates of illness and death from a wide variety of acute and chronic conditions, including cancer, heart attack, and surgery. But men benefit more than women. "If you are a man," Dr. Taylor writes, "the very best thing that you can do for your health is to get married and stay married. It increases the chances of living past age sixty-five from 65 percent to over 90 percent. If you're a woman, you may enjoy happiness in marriage, but your life expectancy will not be affected."

In research on widows and widowers, women may have more financial struggles, but, overall, men have a harder time when a spouse dies. Widowed men are much more likely to remarry. And it isn't just because they have more available partners, although that is true. In her practice, says Ms. Carter, "the wives say that if something happened to their husbands they'd never get married again—it was just too much trouble. Meanwhile, with a man, it's lucky if he waits fifteen minutes after his wife dies to get married, because he needs a caretaker. No way do they feel they can grow old alone."

In contrast, it's rare for a woman to rely completely on her partner. Even when we have significant emotional support from them, we also turn to family and friends. And our partners look—to us. They also rely on us for much, much more. As Lola puts it, "Our division of labor was I did the work, and Jim decided our position on Red China and took care of the yard." Even in relationships that aren't quite so traditional, many of us still shoulder more housework, child care, and social scheduling. We also frequently manage family crises and events. No wonder marriage is so good for men's health.

In contrast, the extra burden has consequences for us. One study of working men and women found that performing more than 46 percent of the total domestic chores increased depressive symptoms. Because women so frequently bear primary responsibility for household tasks, the researchers concluded that inequities in domestic labor may lead to symptoms of depression in working wives.

We also tend to take our problems with our spouses to heart and suffer more from marital conflict. Depression is perhaps the most obvious result, but there are also physiological effects. In one study of cardiovascular disease, just recalling conflict was enough to raise women's blood pressure. In their review of studies of "marital problem discussions" published in the last decade, psychologists Janice K. Kiecolt-Glaser, Ph.D., and Tamara L. Newton, Ph.D., concluded, "Across these studies, the relationships between physiological change and negative behaviors have typically been stronger for women than for men, and women's physiological changes following marital conflict show greater persistence than men's." In other words, we experience more symptoms for longer periods of time.

This finding is in contrast to most other studies of stress. "Typically, men respond to stressful events with greater physiological changes, par-

ticularly in blood pressure, than women do. It is only in this one particular arena—marriage—that they enjoy this striking physiological
protection," writes Dr. Taylor.

Thus, a woman's state of health reflects the state of her marriage.
Not surprisingly, studies have found that we spend more time
thinking about our marriages, reminisce more about important events
in the relationships, and have more detailed and vivid memories of
marital disagreements than do our husbands. We are more sensitive to
conflict, and less insulated from its emotional and physical reverbera-
tions.

What's key, then, to women's health is not just staying married but
staying *happily* married. Fortunately, in our fifties, there's plenty of time
to reconnect, to recognize each other after the turbulent years domi-
nated by children and careers. Whether through compromise, coun-

seling, or finding new activities (or rekindling old ones) that we love
to do together, many of us make profound changes in our relationships
and in the process renew our commitment to our marriages.

TAKING STOCK AND MOVING FORWARD

∞ Why do you think your marriage has lasted? What do you like
most about it? Tell your mate. Are there ways you'd like it to be different? Talk to your partner about this, too.

∞ What interests do you and your partner share? Would you like to
spend more time together as a couple? What kinds of things do you
want to do? Hiking? Traveling? Ballroom dancing?

* Do you and your partner allow each other enough time to pursue individual interests? Do you encourage his? Do you want more time for yourself? How can you make this happen?

* Distance grows between two people when they don't share what's going on in their lives. Do you and your partner regularly talk, call, leave notes? Are you able to joke and laugh together? Are you affectionate with each other? Do you make love regularly?

* How do you and your partner make decisions? Do you feel that both of your needs are taken into account, or does one of you compromise more frequently than the other? What can you do about this?

* List the things you love about your mate, then the things that drive you crazy. Go over the second list to see what can be put in the "not really important" category. Address the things that do matter.

* Do you and your partner have conflicts that simply linger on without resolution? Consider couples therapy.

going it alone

divorce and widowhood

> *"To the extent that we have control over our lives, I feel that I do. I also know that there's a place where control is an illusion. There're some things in life that everyone has to deal with; they come at unpredictable times, and you have to be prepared to respond."*
>
> ——Marlene

THE DAY AFTER OUR thirty-fifth reunion, I met some high school friends for brunch. Of the seven of us, four were divorced (or about to be), and of the four, two had been divorced twice. Why was I surprised? I knew the familiar statistics: Half of first marriages end in divorce, and the rate for remarriages is even higher. There are more than one million divorces in this country every year. Today, unlike earlier times, more marriages end in divorce than in death. Yet attaching those black-and-white numbers to the old friends sitting around the table made the statistics all too real.

On the Holmes-Rahe scale, the gold standard for stress assessment, divorce ranks second only to losing a spouse. And for fifty-something women, it has become a big issue. In the 1990s, for the first time, there were more divorcees than widows among older women. Among women in their late fifties and early sixties, more than 14 percent were divorced as of 1998, up from nearly 4 percent in 1965 and almost 10 percent in 1990. (These figures don't include the many women who are separated.)

When a marriage breaks up, there are no rituals in place to help us learn to live in what writer Andre Dubus called the "foreign land" of divorce. Shortly after my husband left, a friend e-mailed me: "This must be harder than the death of a mate, because you don't receive the condolences and flowers and casseroles and warm reminiscences from friends that you would have if the husband you loved had died. But even so, your friends are grieving for you and the girls, even though there aren't great cultural institutions for demonstrating it."

In fact, some women, at least for a while, wish that they had been widowed. Take Natalie, whose husband left her for another woman. "I used to think if he'd died, it would have been easier because I wouldn't have to run into him. I was always afraid of that."

Not only did my ex stay in town, but because he is a well-known writer, I had to confront his byline, and sometimes his picture, in the newspaper every week. Particularly wrenching were those articles where he mentioned dining or vacationing with his "companion." And since we had children, there was no avoiding continuing contact. For the first year, I was too upset to even talk to him on the phone.

Even so, our children do help us through. "If you have children, there's a reason to go on," says Natalie, who has no kids. "I used to wake up every day, my stomach would take a nosedive, and I'd think, 'Oh God, here I am again. Why can't I just die in my sleep?'"

Enduring the end of a long-term marriage is harrowing, whether it has come about through divorce or widowhood. (Although we don't think of widowhood as a common event during our fifties, the average age of widows in the United States is fifty-six.) So much is happening at this time, even under normal circumstances, that divorce and widowhood are frequently simultaneous with other life-changing events. "To deal with getting divorced in the middle of your life—and menopause, letting go of your kids, having nobody to fall back on, feeling your mortality, all those things that hit women in our age group—is incredibly hard," says Bonnie, who is now in a committed relationship. Looking around the rubble of a failed marriage, we learn the terrible lesson that security is ephemeral, and the companionship we came to take for granted is no more.

In addition to companionship, we may need someone else (usually a partner) to validate our experiences. In *Towards a New Psychology of Women*, psychiatrist Jean Baker Miller, M.D., explains, "Unless there is another person present, the entire event—the thought, the feeling, the accomplishment, or whatever it may be—lacks pleasure and significance." For more than a year after my husband left, every time I went someplace interesting, did something fun, read something of note, I wanted to tell him about it, to share it and make it real. It felt like I was dragging around a phantom limb. How do we build our sense of self when we're suddenly alone?

Besides, being on our own is frightening. Even with friends and family nearby, it's not the same as having a partner. "If I get lost, if anything happens, there's only me," says Natalie. "There's nobody at home who's going to notice or be concerned. It's a strange and lonely feeling, even though my family is all around." I know just what she means. When I needed outpatient surgery, my daughters and friends provided transportation, food, and TLC. Still, I felt single, alone, and worried.

Even when women initiate the divorce, we don't escape these consequences. For Marsha, who left her husband three years ago, it's been difficult. "There were times I felt so alone and so lonely I would call a friend and say, 'I don't think I'm going to make it until morning.'"

The rule of thumb for recovery from divorce is five years. What makes it especially hard is that the road to feeling better is neither straight nor steady; it's a circuitous path with some ups and many downs. Of course, we expect holidays, anniversaries, birthdays, and other family occasions to be tough. But we are surprised when a fragment of a song on the radio makes us burst into tears.

As novelist Elizabeth Buchan wrote in *The Revenge of the Middle-Aged Woman*, we do get glimpses of feeling better: "Then I heard it. Click. Click. For a second or two, my mind slipped free of the net in which it was caught and I glimpsed the prospect of release, a future where I would be empty and clean. It was the cool, fresh wind blowing through a sickroom." Likewise, I remember marveling to myself, "I haven't cried in a week." Then, we spiral back down into devastating grief. Not too long ago, during yet another bad period, my therapist told me, "It's not the depth of the descent that matters, it's how quickly you rebound." He was right; I felt better in a few days. Still, progress was painfully bumpy and slow.

According to Shelley E. Taylor, Ph.D., professor of psychology at UCLA, separated and divorced people are more vulnerable to depression. Compared with married people, they get sick more and for longer periods, they make 30 percent more visits to doctors, they are more likely to become chronically ill and disabled, and they are more susceptible to infectious diseases, especially fatal ones. On the other hand, they also frequently seek therapy, which is often a lifeline to recovery.

behind the statistics

At midlife, the story is all too familiar: the long-term marriage that breaks up when the husband leaves for another (often younger) woman. So what lies behind this familiar tale? According to Maria Tupper, a clinical social worker in private practice, "Even adults have developmental work to do. In each relationship of your life, you're completing the work of another stage. When someone 'falls out of love' it usually has more to do with being discontent themselves, and they project that onto their partner. Being with a new person is a way of getting fulfillment and escaping that dissatisfaction."

Often, the breakup of a long-term marriage is the culmination of a slow process. "There's a gradual and pernicious breakdown in communication," says Rona Ahrens, a psychotherapist in private practice. "I tell people, 'You talk in English, your partner hears it in Italian and responds in Greek, and you hear the response in Arabic.' Then emotion takes over, and what's being said doesn't matter." Unresolved conflicts go under the rug, taking on a life of their own.

The gender issue also plays its part. Says Ms. Ahrens, "I hate to generalize, but women have more tenacious memories. They can tell you the date and time that he did x, y, or z. Men are more out to lunch. The guy feels he can't win because she's got the facts, so what's he going to do, hit her? The men become mute, and that's symptom number one, a huge red flag."

Women compound the problem, says family therapist Betty Carter, by making the "pursuer-distancer" mistake. "The more she asks, 'How do you feel?' the more he retreats, because men have been trained to think that only wimps talk about their feelings. When I see wives and husbands separately, I tell the wives, 'Don't ask him how he feels. Ask him what he thinks. Then he'll tell you how he feels.'"

"Intimacy" may be another red flag—or red herring—in signaling trouble. Ms. Carter says men and women understand that word differently. "Men think sex is being intimate, so they ask, 'What else do you want?' Women say, 'I want someone to talk to me, and I want to talk to you.' One of the classic stalemates—and by the way, a stalemate is 'useful' because no one has to change—is this: He says, 'If we had more sex, we'd have a better relationship,' and she says, 'If we had a better relationship, we'd have more sex.'" Who can achieve intimacy when we can't even agree on how to define it?

Some couples confuse intimacy with "fusion," which, as Ms. Carter explains, "is a two-headed person; everything is 'we.' Typically, one partner needs to be with the other in order to feel okay." In contrast, when both partners are mature and have enough self-esteem, they can achieve true intimacy, which, she says, is "two separate people deciding and freely giving attention and love to each other."

After my marriage broke up, I was shocked by the number of close friends who told me I was a different person, someone they liked much better out of the couple. Like many other "smug marrieds," as Bridget Jones would say, I'd lost the habit of seeing myself as an individual. Hard as it's been to accept, I've realized that I allowed myself to be submerged in the relationship, what a fellow divorcee calls "going underground."

Of course, there are bad marriages and mismatches. Sometimes a major life change, such as the death of a child, breaks up the marriage. Or marriages may be more fragile now, as both partners navigate individual life changes. There may not be much left, either, if we've spent years raising children or pursuing our careers. Diana, for one, had put all her energy into her work; when she lost her prestigious job in advertising she realized her marriage was an empty shell: "I had power, the corner office, and a high salary. When that was all gone, and it was just me and my husband, I noticed for the first time we were strangers. We weren't talking and we didn't have any common interests." Diana and her husband decided that their marriage was too far gone, so they divorced, although they remain friends.

As both men and women proceed through our fifties, we realize that there is limited time left to live out our fantasies, so we may be tempted to stray. But for men, especially successful ones, the opportunities for extramarital affairs are readily available. One of my happily married male friends travels frequently for work. He's told me how easy it would be, if he were so inclined, to hook up with women on the road, in airports, or in hotels. (My ex, by the way, met his girlfriend on an airplane.) "Young women are aggressive about flirting, especially if a man has money," says Ms. Ahrens. "They don't care if he is married. And nothing is fresh after twenty-five years, so if a man has sex with someone new, he feels reborn." When one or both partners are not willing to put in the effort necessary to get through a rough period, a chance sexual encounter may develop into an escape route.

Women are also tempted to experiment. Worried that we are becoming less attractive (paralleling a man's worry about potency), we may feel that this is our last chance to have a romantic or sexual adventure. Still, more often than not, when women leave a marriage, it's not because there's another man in the picture. "My experience is that men, particularly in middle age, will not leave their wives without another woman in the offing," Ms. Ahrens says, "but women leave now because they can support themselves."

Indeed, women initiate—that is, serve the papers—in two-thirds of divorces. According to "The Top Ten Myths of Divorce" from the National Marriage Project at Rutgers University, "The higher rate of women initiators is probably due to the fact that men are more likely . . . to have problems with drinking, drug abuse, and infidelity."

But there's more to it than that. In our parents' day, most wives were financially dependent on their husbands. Today, we are approaching a more egalitarian model. We expect to contribute to the family finances, and we also expect companionship, love, and emotional support. Hilarie Lieb, Ph.D., of the department of economics at Northwestern University, points out, "Because women feel more financially independent, they have more bargaining power in a relationship. If it's not a financial bond, they can ask, 'Why are we together?' As a consequence, other factors take on relatively more importance."

In addition, in many states, thanks to no-fault divorce and a shift toward what's called "equitable settlement," women today are not as frightened about the financial repercussions of divorce. The upshot, says Roberta Friedman, a divorce lawyer and mediator in New Haven, Connecticut, is that "women get to their forties and fifties and say to their husbands, 'I don't want to grow old with you; I don't want to take care of you.' They're looking for more than someone to make dinner for or go out with on Saturday night. They honestly feel as though they could have a more satisfying life without this person. Often the men are shocked and clueless about why the wife wants out. And they're angry because, in most cases, they'll be asked to help support the wife and/or the children."

the business of divorce

It's a lot easier to get married than it is to get divorced. Divorce is more than an emotional matter; it's also a legal and economic proposition.

It reduces a long-term, intimate relationship to a list of assets and liabilities, and can turn a partner into an adversary.

Like many couples, my husband and I chose mediation because it was a less expensive way to go. Besides, we agreed about custody, and we felt we could resolve the financial issues relatively easily. However, mediation does not always offer a level playing field because some women are unprepared to stand up for their due. According to *Our Turn*, which describes the "Divorce after 40" study done by the National Center for Women and Retirement Research, more than 40 percent of women worried more about "being fair" than about their own needs.

In addition to wanting to be fair, we might have been raised to be "good girls" and have a hard time expressing our needs. Ms. Friedman observes, "Women in this age group are often not adept at advocating for themselves. I find myself reframing or reposing questions in order to give the woman the opportunity to say something without making her husband angry." For example, in a discussion of alimony, she might repeat the question, "Are you both sure there's no need for a minimum monthly payment?" Anxious and frightened, we may not be skilled negotiators. Besides, men often have more experience at the bargaining table, even when they don't have jobs that involve negotiating skills.

When mediation won't work, the divorce lawyers enter the picture, and things can get ugly and expensive. Sarah Eldrich, an attorney in New Haven, Connecticut, explains, "There's a saying that criminal lawyers see the worst people at their best and divorce lawyers see the best people at their worst." It makes sense. The stakes are awfully high, and the emotions are raw. Husbands still usually earn more than their wives, even in dual career marriages. Of course, there are exceptions, but most women face some financial uncertainty. According to the

"Working Woman's Guide to Financial Security," women fifty and older experience a 39 percent drop in income immediately following divorce, while men undergo only a 14 percent decline. One year after divorce, only 21 percent of women have regained their predivorce income; the comparable figure for men is 40 percent. In the "Divorce after 40" study, 88 percent of the women had money worries in the first year. Five years later, money was still a major concern for seven out of ten.

Medical benefits are another worry. "More often than not, I'd say 90 percent of the time, even if the wife has a job, it's a job without benefits, and the husband carries the insurance," says Ms. Friedman. Bonnie, for example, enjoyed being a freelance consultant, but after her divorce, she took a job at one of the places where she consulted. "I had such a dread fear: 'If I get sick, how will I support myself?' I needed a regular income and health insurance," she says. It can be difficult and expensive for midlife women to get health insurance, and we are too young for Medicare, which kicks in at age sixty-five.

Scarier still is retirement. Even women who have worked full-time are at a disadvantage. Explains Heidi Hartmann, Ph.D., president and CEO of the Institute for Women's Policy Research, "In general, the pension gap is bigger than the wage gap. Many women have spent time out of the labor market to raise children. On average, women earn 75 percent of what men do. But if you've only been working half the number of years, your pension will be only 35 percent of what a man would get." For the same reason, our Social Security benefits are also lower. In 1999, for example, women received an average of $697 a month, while men received an average of $904.

Once divorced, we have to take care of ourselves. And sadly, when it comes to finances, we may have a lot to learn. Even professional women, like Natalie, sometimes cede financial decision making to their partners. "He paid all the bills, so he'd tell me how much money to give him every month. Honestly, I wouldn't have known what the electric bill was. I had no idea."

My ex-husband and I had a more equal role in our day-to-day finances. But I did buy into his ideas about retirement, a decision I now regret. "I'm going to be working forever, so you don't have to worry," he always said, justifying our fairly minimal contributions to a retirement plan. Oops! Now, I figure *I'll* be working forever. At least I won't be alone. According to an article in the *New York Times* in 2001, "hundreds of thousands" of women in their sixties are forced to stay in the workforce because they can't afford to retire.

Unfortunately, we sometimes make huge decisions when we are, to put it bluntly, basket cases. Natalie badly wanted out of her marriage, and she didn't have the energy to fight. "On paper it looked like I made more money than he did, but he had an antique collection worth more than $300,000. My lawyer thought I should have everything appraised and go to court, but I was afraid. I had signed every tax form, so I was liable for all those years of his business, even though I wasn't involved in it. I didn't want my life tied up, so I decided it wasn't worth it. I did get the house, but otherwise, I'm starting from scratch."

Finances are also a big issue for widows, especially when their husbands handled the money. Soon after being widowed at age fifty-two, Gail had to declare bankruptcy after losing all her money in a business partnership with an unscrupulous contractor. "I had been pretty astute about money and I'd always been able to take care of myself. Had I really been thinking clearly after my husband died, I would have done things differently."

the innocent bystanders

Whether we've been left or have done the leaving, we worry about how our children will weather this dreadful upheaval. It's very tough, especially at the beginning. Stunned by the worst pain I'd ever experienced, I still had to be available for my daughters, who were reeling from their own feelings of shock, grief, and betrayal. I knew the worst thing I could do was to put them in the middle, but it was impossible to disguise my hurt and anger at their father.

Too often, we may have to bite our tongues to keep from badmouthing our exes. Bonnie's husband left her for one of his graduate students. When the new girlfriend turned thirty, her twenty-year-old son said, "I'm so glad my father doesn't have a girlfriend in her twenties anymore." What was Bonnie to say?

When divorce occurs at midlife, our children are more likely to be older. If we're lucky, we're not in for major battles over custody. Still, divorce can make us dread holidays, graduations, and other family occasions, no matter what the ages of our kids. Even when there are clear agreements about where they will spend their time, our children often experience conflicting loyalties. And we suffer, too.

I'll never forget the first Thanksgiving I spent without my children. Although I'd had the holiday at my house each year since the divorce, I decided to accept an invitation to a friend's house. My daughters were welcome to come with me, but they each decided to go elsewhere: Kate spent the day with her dad and his girlfriend's family; Emma went to a friend's house. All three of us were miserable, and we vowed to spend Thanksgiving together in the future.

Even when things go as smoothly as they can, children still feel the effects. Bonnie's marriage broke up when her son was a junior in high school. "He fell apart academically. He just couldn't concentrate. He ended up in a good school, but he had been the hardworking Harvard-bound type. It was bad timing."

But there is no such thing as good timing. You might think that the older the children, the better. Yet, divorce may be particularly difficult for children who are in college or getting ready to leave home. Ms. Tupper observes, "It's very unsettling for older kids. The solid base they've come to count on has shifted, just as they're heading out." It's especially hard for kids if the divorce necessitates selling the family home. In addition, our own straitened budgets may not allow us to give them financial help if they need it. If they lose a job, break up with a boyfriend, or run into other trouble, they may not feel they have a place to retreat to. Sociologist Frances Goldscheider, Ph.D., who does research on adult children at Brown University, adds, "One of our more poignant findings is how much less likely are the children of divorce to return home. They don't have as much access to a safety net. And you can't leap without a safety net underneath."

In addition, adult children may find themselves in the uncomfortable position of having to take sides. "Very often they become overly involved in the divorce and aligned with one parent or the other," says Ms. Friedman. "I've never found a party to a divorce who's admitted trying to influence a child, but often it happens."

For our children, divorce raises questions about trust and relationships. My daughters had grown up in a stable, happy family. Suddenly (at least in their eyes), it fell apart. It pains me now to hear how skeptical they are about relationships with men.

Even as *we* heal, we may be causing *them* more pain—or at least very mixed feelings. Two years after my marriage broke up, I got involved with a man. My younger daughter said, "It's so hard to watch your parents date." On the other hand, Bonnie says of her son, "I heard him say to my friend, 'My mom is really depressed; she needs to be dating.'" If either or both parents get involved with someone new, logistics can get tricky. The adolescent daughter of a divorced friend has three bedrooms: one at her father's condo, and one each at her mom's and her mom's boyfriend's houses.

Still, as we recover, we can take comfort in knowing that we're empowering our children by modeling strong, healthy behavior. And we may emerge from the ordeal closer to them than we were before. "Children stay closer to parents, particularly if they are divorced, and they especially tend to be closer to their mothers," says Debra Umberson, Ph.D., a sociologist at the University of Texas in Austin.

the generation gap

Divorce can also create tension in our relationships with our parents, since it bore a stigma in their generation. The biggest scandal of my childhood was when the next-door neighbors divorced. Many of our parents still live in that mind-set. They know the numbers, but divorce is not supposed to happen to their children, and they may feel ashamed, dismayed, or disapproving.

Parents tend to see the divorce through their own lens, and that infuriates us. When I told my parents the news, my mother asked about the sordid details of my husband's affair. I'm sure she was just curious and upset, but I was enraged. We're made to feel as if we've let them down just when we most need support. Diana's mother's reaction was, "How can you do this to me?"

I'm not saying that this isn't hard for our parents, or that they don't care. As a parent myself, I know how terrible it is to watch helplessly when your child is hurt. Our parents worry about us and their grandchildren, and they don't want to see us suffer. My parents were concerned about my finances. Besides, when my seemingly model marriage turned out to be an illusion, one of their greatest pleasures vanished.

Of course, many parents come through, emotionally and financially. Natalie's parents "were right there for me. They kept calling me, asking me out to dinner. They'd rejoice anytime I had a date. And the first thing they asked was, 'Do you need money?'"

But as Erica, divorced and on her own, discovered, accepting financial help is complicated. "My parents gave me money. It wasn't that they couldn't spare it, but on some level, my mother was always mad at me, even though she kept it underground. Last year I stopped taking their money, and our relationship has improved ten thousand percent."

a friend in need . . .

Parents may provide support, but it's usually our friends who get us through. Says Natalie, "Everyone was calling me, rallying around, even people I hadn't seen in a year."

In my case, every friend found some way to help. Some called or e-mailed every day. Others came through with frequent dinner invitations, or they made sure I got out to movies or plays, hikes and bike rides. One close friend, whose strong point is not day-to-day contact, let me know that I could call her anytime and that she'd spend the night on a moment's notice if I couldn't face being alone. My oldest friends, a couple I've known since college, live out of town, and I escaped to their house on occasional weekends. They let me be a zombie, they cooked for me, they talked to me (or didn't). It felt like going home, when my own home was unbearably empty.

When a bullet strikes a marriage, its ricochet is felt throughout the couple's circle of friends. Especially if the breakup is hostile, friends divide into his-or-her camps. I stayed closer with most of our mutual friends because my ex had been the "bad boy." Still, there are people I care about whom I no longer see.

Some friends find it hard to handle the intensity of our pain. Or they are forced into an unwelcome reappraisal of their own marriages. One close friend had often thought about leaving her husband; seeing my anguish convinced her to stay. Women who had never doubted their husbands experienced a shiver of fear when they heard what my ex had been up to. After all, we'd seemed so content. Other friends may even become envious when we recover and explore new relationships with men.

Some friends move closer to the center, while others drift to the periphery of our lives. Deepening intimacy may be a welcome surprise in some friendships, as Erica found. "I was accustomed to being the caregiver. But I learned to lean on my women friends, to depend on them, to let their strength hold me up in a way that I never had before. It was hard exposing myself and revealing my weakness. Yet, it was totally rewarding. There was an element of wonderment, that this was part of our friendship, too."

If we've traveled in the world of couples, we may lose married friends because it's awkward to relate as a group of three instead of the familiar foursome. A new, uncomfortable ambiguity may emerge with married male friends. Also, we may feel that our coupled friends don't understand what we're going through. "Singleness becomes the elephant in the room," says Stephanie, who remains single since her divorce fifteen years ago. "They see you as single, but they don't know what that means. They don't think, 'Gee, what's it like not to have sex for a year, or to have no one to cuddle with? What's it like not to have plans on a Saturday night?'"

Weekends are especially difficult for divorced women. When you're in a couple, even if you haven't scheduled weekend activities, there's always someone around to watch that video or just hang out. Not if you're single. "Now, if I don't make plans, it doesn't happen and I'm by myself," says Marsha. Even with a close woman friend, there's an unspoken assumption that her marriage comes first. As Stephanie observes, "The relationship with her partner is the most important, and you will always be second. She needs to have time with her husband, she has to get off the phone because he needs to talk to her, or she can't go to this movie because she promised her husband." On the other hand, your married friends may struggle with guilt when they don't include you in their plans.

Finding single friends improves our situation. Says Erica, "Single people, especially if they don't have kids, can get up and go anytime. I can go out every night if I want to."

getting back on the horse

Venturing into dating may not be easy at first. We may hope our friends will fix us up, but it doesn't happen as frequently as we expect, as in Erica's case. "I have a lot of friends and I got fixed up once—with the only single man anyone knew." Yet, it's another story for men. Says Stephanie, "People tell me they don't know anyone for me. But when a man becomes single, he's fixed up in a second."

Enter the online dating services. Ten percent of the members of Match.com, for example, are over fifty. Some of us approach this tentatively, but Diana took it on as a project: "I had some money stashed away, so I took six months out of my business. I methodically searched the profiles of every single man." She eventually met someone she dated for more than two years. Now she's back online, still hoping to find a long-term relationship.

Still, the pickings are slim. Some of the middle-aged men listed on-line have never been in a long-term relationship; I've been warned about them. In addition, most men tend to "date down," especially in second and third marriages. According to data from Match.com, men between the ages of fifty and fifty-four want to date a forty-three-year-old woman; those between fifty-five and fifty-nine are looking for a woman around forty-seven.

It's the older men who want *us*. Men between sixty and sixty-four are looking for a fifty-one-year-old, while men age sixty-five dream of that perfect fifty-four-year-old woman. "It was so jarring when I realized that the men who wanted to go out with me were sixty," says Bonnie.

In contrast, we tend to look for men our own age. Despite her company's data, Match.com's Trish McDermott, vice president of ro-mance (no, I'm not kidding), thinks that women may be missing an opportunity. "Women assume that men five, ten, or fifteen years younger will not want to date them. We all want to limit the rejec-tions we experience. But I've been in the dating business a long time, and I see a little shift. Men are more willing to date up."

We're in for some culture shock when we start dating. Customs have shifted since we were last out there—or have they? In the post–women's liberation world, there's a lot of confusion about how to behave. For example, says Ms. McDermott, "if he pays for the date, does that suggest he has a sexual expectation? How sexual are you sup-posed to be on the first date? If you let the man buy dinner, are you suggesting that you can't pay for dinner, or that you're an old-fash-ioned girl? Because you're not, you're a corporate CEO."

Some men feel threatened if we're accomplished and well-off. Says Stephanie, "The relationship of men and women around power hasn't changed, and it complicates the field. My old boyfriend got uptight about money if I wanted to go to a nice restaurant. I didn't care if I paid. It didn't make me feel like I didn't want to sleep with him. But he cared. It affected how he felt about himself."

For those of us whose husbands walked out, there's an additional wrinkle. Stephanie adds, "There's always that veil of being the 'left one,' that there was something about you that made them leave."

Alas, we are strangers in a strange land. We may be in our fifties, but we feel like awkward teenagers. In fact, I've endured the humiliation of asking my daughters for advice: Who calls who, how many days do you wait before calling, and how do you say no in a nice way? Erica finds it even more confusing. "It's like being all the ages you've ever been, all at once. You're a teenager, you're a person in her twenties, you're acting like you're thirty and forty and fifty."

Still, we can learn, says Ms. McDermott. "I firmly believe dating is a skill we perfect with practice, like reading. People who've been in a couple for a long time have to brush off their rusty dating skills. With practice, dating becomes less about 'How am I screwing up?' or 'Is there broccoli in my teeth?' You can concentrate on having fun, and we are our most attractive when we're having fun."

Still, the best dating skills may not prepare us for everything. Like a lot of us, Stephanie has her share of dating horror stories, but here's one with a particularly modern twist. "The worst was when a friend fixed me up with someone who turned out to be gay. He actually brought his partner along! At dinner, I bent to pick up my napkin and I saw him fondling the guy's knee." Perhaps the best advice is this, from one of my more experienced friends: "Take a deep breath, hold your nose, and jump in."

If we're lucky enough to meet someone, the prospect of sexual intimacy is thrilling. Stephanie says, "It's hard as a single, aging person to hold on to your own sexuality by yourself. When I'm going out with someone and I think they're interested in me, I feel so much sexier." Of course, there's "the talk" about HIV/AIDS to get through first, and our ignorance can get us into trouble. Bonnie got involved with a man who told her he had had herpes and couldn't use a condom. "I didn't know what that meant. He said he'd know if he was going to have an outbreak and he'd tell me." As a result of her naïveté, she now has the herpes virus in her blood. "I didn't know the stuff that any twenty-year-old does," she says. As Erica explains, "There's no way to have that talk except to have it: Have you been tested, who have you been sleeping with, how safe am I with you, how safe are you with me?" It gets easier the second or third time, she adds.

In addition, after years of relying on our husbands for reassurance that we are still attractive, many of us are anxious about facing a new partner. "When I took a hard look at what my body looked like," says Diana, "it was 'Oh God, what will I do?'" Taking the plunge, though, was worth it, she adds. "With my new boyfriend, I had the best sex I've ever had. It felt like everything was working."

Many of us do find that sex with someone new is especially exciting, thanks to the novelty and stimulation of a new partner. And let's not forget that in long-term marriages, repressed resentment or boredom often dampens sexual ardor. Newly single women may take heart from this finding from a study done by Paul Gebhard, Ph.D., while director of the Kinsey Institute of Sex Research: "The percentage of women reaching orgasm in virtually every coital act is higher for both the widowed and divorced than it is for married women." In addition, he wrote, "the gradual increase with age in the proportion of divorcees reaching orgasm (nine times out of ten or better) suggests a rebound in responsiveness depressed by an unhappy marital situation."

The world of dating is a roller coaster, and the results are decidedly mixed. Bonnie is happily talking about setting up a home with the man she's been seeing. "I'm in the quieter stages of being in love with him; we're past that initial manick-y high, but I feel really alive." On the other hand, Erica has been through several boyfriends since she left her husband five years ago, and she's still looking. "I'd like to have a long-term relationship, and I'd like it to happen before I'm sixty."

Some of us decide that dating isn't worth it. For Marsha, if it happens, it happens. "I would like someone to hang out with, but I don't want to date. I find it too demeaning, at my age, to be all aflutter about whether somebody likes me. Besides, I'm very independent; I'm not someone who thinks that you're nothing without a man."

It may be different for widows, however, especially if their marriages were happy. When her husband died, Gail had no interest in dating; nor does she ever expect to have as close a relationship in her life. Still, two years after her husband died, she got involved with an old friend. She views it philosophically. "I like the companionship and we get along well. But my husband was my soul mate."

giving marriage another try?

Many middle-aged divorced women do not want to remarry or even live with a man again. I'm not sure I do. Sure, it'd be great to have a regular companion for social events, but we no longer want to compromise our privacy and freedom by living with a man.

Once we adjust to the loss of sharing a life with someone, we begin to relish living alone. In the "Divorce after 40" study, 46 percent of the women between fifty and fifty-nine said they'd prefer to remain single. "I call my ideal man the 'New York boyfriend,'" says Marlene, who lives in New Jersey. "I visit him, I have a great place to stay, and then I get back on the train. It's companionship on demand. I don't need or want to be 24/7. I have a pretty full life, and whoever this is, he has to fit into *my* lifestyle."

In any case, the odds are against us. The older women get, the less likely we are to remarry. Statistically, we're at a disadvantage because as we age, there are more women than men. Among thirty-five- to fifty-four-year-olds, there are 105 unmarried women for every 100 unmarried men. But among people fifty-five and older, the ratio increases to 291 unmarried women for every 100 unmarried men.

Even if we do marry again, the likelihood of divorce is higher than for a first marriage. And if there are children involved, tackling the problems of a so-called blended or "reconstituted" family is no picnic. Those of us remarrying at midlife are likely to be dealing with children who are old enough to have strong feelings about their parents' divorce and remarriage as well as about the new "parent." "The situations that don't work out are the ones where the stepparent wants to be treated like a mother or father and isn't respectful of the blood parent," explains Ms. Tupper. In other words, we need to act like an additional parent, rather than the "new mom."

Finances can also be complicated, emotionally and otherwise. Older children of wealthy parents may have serious reservations because they're afraid of losing their inheritance. We may have to take account of alimony or child support, multiple households, and previous debt. Making wills and deciding which children get what is also an issue.

If we haven't had children of our own, becoming a stepmother in midlife carries with it a whole new host of issues. It can be a boon or a disappointment. Pat, who never expected to have children of her own, married a man who had eight children and twelve grandchildren. "When I married him, I thought I'd feel a strong connection with them, but for some reason I don't. Did I throw my maternal feelings out the window?"

Gail's experience was just the opposite. At forty-three, with no children of her own, she married her third husband, who had children from his previous marriages. "I have been blessed. I have three stepchildren who are wonderful. We are truly close. Even since their father died, we stay in touch, I see the grandkids, and I am included in all their family functions."

Besides the children, there are other relatives to consider—parents, grandparents, ex-in-laws, whew! No wonder it's so hard to make blended families work. According to Betty Carter, it takes three to five years for things to calm down and everyone to settle into these new relationships.

it's getting better

However we choose to live, surviving divorce is an enormous test of personal strength, but we often emerge happier than we were before. Even those of us who were "dumped" often come to feel that no marriage is better than a bad one. "I knew for a long time that it felt oppressive to be with him," says Bonnie. "Part of me knew I should leave, but another part knew I never would. So the fact that he bailed out—well, somebody should have."

When our marriages end, we have to give up the idea that someone else is responsible for our happiness or unhappiness. We confront the realization that we have no partner there to take care of us.

Accepting these truths is hard; yet doing so gives us the power and confidence to shape our own lives. We learn that we can tackle anything that comes along. Newly divorced or widowed women may learn to do their taxes, take a more active role in household repairs, manage their finances on their own. The first winter I was alone, a small but significant watershed was setting mousetraps in the basement and garage, something my husband had always done. Ugh. More formidable accomplishments included being a single mom in a weeklong summer rental on the Cape with my younger daughter and her friend, refinancing my house, and buying a car—things I had previously done in partnership with my ex. Hard as it is, taking on new responsibilities builds our sense of mastery.

In the "Divorce after 40" study, nearly two-thirds of the women said that divorce inspired them to gain control over their lives for the first time. They went back to school, started new jobs, and renewed their social lives. They redefined themselves and reawakened their own hopes and dreams. The vast majority—80 percent—emerged with a more positive self-image and higher self-esteem.

Let's give ourselves credit: It's an enormous achievement to extricate ourselves from "coupleness," to discover our individual strengths and become autonomous human beings, to learn to enter into relationships as adults, with adults. This is especially true if we played the supporting role to a man with a more dominant personality or if, like me, we submerged our identity in the couple. If we're successful, divorce gives us the chance to become ourselves. As Natalie says, "I had no confidence for several years after the divorce. Now, I have more confidence in myself than I ever did. I feel sure about who I am and where I want to go, what route I want to take. I make my own choices in life."

Taking Stock and Moving Forward

❧ It's said that grief is a spiral; we revisit the source of our pain again and again, from a different place each time. When grief engulfs you, do you bounce back more quickly as time goes on? Or do you get stuck in mourning your lost relationship? If so, consider counseling.

❧ Do you feel lonely without the built-in social life you've been accustomed to? Making sure that you schedule dates with friends at least a few times a week can help. So can entertaining. Is there a class, a lecture or concert series, or a theater subscription you might try?

❧ Are you concerned about your financial security? Do you need to bring in more money? Networking with colleagues, former colleagues, and friends can help, as can a session with a financial planner.

❧ Are you dating, or thinking about it? Do you have concerns about sexually transmitted diseases? Talking to your gynecologist can help you clarify the risks and decide how to proceed.

❧ Do you have people you can rely on in a crisis? If you need a doctor? If the power goes out? If not, come to an understanding with a close friend or a sibling that he or she will be there for you in an emergency.

motherhood

daring decisions, delights, and difficulties

> *"There is no medical reason that healthy women in their 50s should be prevented from having babies with donated eggs, the largest study of motherhood after menopause has found."*
>
> —Associate Press article in the *New York Times*, November 13, 2002
>
> *"Do you know why a 55-year-old woman shouldn't have a child? She'd forget where she put it."*
>
> —Stephanie, age 55

WHEN I BEGAN WRITING this book, the chapter on children was going to be solely about the "empty nest." Well, Toto, we're not in Kansas anymore. Of course, the number of women in their fifties having babies is tiny. According to the Centers for Disease Control and Prevention, there were 255 births nationwide to women between the ages of fifty and fifty-four in 2000, and they don't even track births to women over age fifty-four.

But many women *do* delay having children. According to the National Center for Health Statistics, between 1970 and 2000, the average age of mothers for all births increased three years, from twenty-four to twenty-seven. Meanwhile, birth rates for women in their thirties and forties have risen. Translation: Not only did we wait longer to have our first children, but we continued having babies later in our lives. So, even in our fifties, some of us are parenting youngsters.

The series of studies of the Radcliffe class of 1969 reflects the variety of choices we've made. When researchers revisited the women in 1990, they found that the age of the oldest child (including stepchildren) ranged from one year to thirty. The youngest children were anywhere between one and seventeen years old.

Some studies have shown that during midlife, women whose children have left home have a higher level of well-being and a lower incidence of depression than women living with young children. So how do the demands of raising youngsters jibe with the other changes occurring as we go through our fifties?

It isn't always easy, but a sense of humor helps, says Laura. After years of struggling with infertility, she and her husband adopted a baby girl from China. (China encourages older adoptive parents; in fact, parents under thirty are not allowed to adopt.) "So here I am at fifty-four, with an eighteen-month-old. I'm having hot flashes, and I'm also a little addled in my thinking. How do I even decide what she should wear today? Other women my age are talking about menopause, and I want to talk about Teletubbies and what's the best diaper ointment." But despite being out of synch with her friends, she has no regrets. "I feel like the hole in my heart has been filled up. It's changed every-thing for me. I have a sense of completeness now, and I didn't even know how incomplete I had been feeling. Bringing this baby girl into our lives is far and away the most satisfying thing I've ever done."

daring decisions

Child-bearing age isn't the only arena where we've broken the mold. Significantly more women in our generation have *not* had children. According to the 2000 census, 19 percent of all women ages forty to forty-four were childless, a figure that's almost doubled since 1980. Turning fifty can be a watershed; if we haven't already done so, we squarely face the reality that motherhood (unless we adopt) is not in the cards.

Some women made a deliberate choice to avoid what David Gut-mann, Ph.D., professor emeritus of psychology at Northwestern Uni-versity, called the "chronic emergency" of parenthood. "I didn't want children and I am very clear why," says Diana. "I didn't have the en-ergy and the focus to always be giving, giving. I don't regret it." On the other hand, Rachel feels she made the decision unconsciously, for which she is sorry. "Now, I wish I had a child. But I do believe that if you want something enough, you go after it. If I had really wanted one, I'd have had one, even if I had to be a single mom."

Even though they were married, several women I talked to felt that had they had a child, they'd have ended up raising it without help from their spouses. "I got to be forty," Natalie says, "and I really wanted to have a baby. But I didn't want to be the sole caretaker of a child, and I knew that was the way it was going to be because my husband was too immersed in himself."

And some women don't meet the right man till late in their reproductive lives, when conception is more difficult. Ellie had put most of her time into her career. She had several long-term relationships but never really settled down. At forty-four, she met and moved in with a man who also wanted children. When they consulted infertility specialists, they were advised against going for treatments, and they were warned that the chance of having a child on their own was only three percent. "We did try, but it didn't work out. Both of us wonder how we let all that time go by." Although she just turned fifty, they're now considering adoption.

Many women without their own children are deeply engaged with other kids, like Marlene, who plays an "auntie" role with several children in her life. Natalie has several nieces and nephews. "I'm very close to them; they're like my own." Ellie and her boyfriend are also involved with nieces and nephews. Yet, she adds, "I still have that little gnawing feeling, I wish I had children, and I have momentary feelings of sadness."

Despite occasional wistfulness, though, most women who wanted children and didn't have them move on without regret. The authors of *Lifeprints*, a book-length study of the lives of 300 midlife women, noted no differences in well-being between mothers and childless women. Moreover, they said, "rarely did women express the kind of deep, wrenching sorrow that childless women are expected to experience, and many expressed no regret at all."

Many of us created alternative families that were nearly unheard of in earlier generations. According to the American Psychiatric Association, estimates of the number of lesbian mothers in this country range from one to five million. Dorothy, who has been in a relationship with Lucy for more than seventeen years, is the adoptive mother of a fourteen-year-old son. She describes the pride she felt during her partner's pregnancy, the result of artificial insemination: "We climbed a mountain together when she was six months pregnant. It was a big moment, emotionally. We were really going to do this, to bring this baby into the world, and everything was going to be okay. All along the way up there were people resting, but we made it to the top. There she was, with her big belly. It was a mad thing we did."

We've also been pioneers of the so-called blended family. Some of us who thought we wouldn't have children find that we have stepchildren, thanks to a couple of decades of exploding rates of divorce and remarriage. Twenty-five years ago, when Ruth married a widower with three young children, whom she later adopted, she was on her own. "It was a painful, difficult experience that I wasn't able to share, and there really were no books at that time. I didn't realize that I was going to have to do far more than a natural mother because I had to convince these children that I was going to be there for them, that I was going to be their mother. And to do that I had to be there 24/7."

When we couldn't find partners, some of us had children alone. Annie had been involved with both men and women, but she wasn't in a long-term relationship. "I thought, if I wait for Mr. Right or even Ms. Right, I might be past childbearing age, so if I'm going to do this, I'm going to do it," she recalls. Fifteen years ago, she was artificially inseminated by an anonymous donor, and today, she is the mother of twins, a daughter and a son.

Of course, these new and unconventional choices have consequences. Infertility treatments, such as IVF (in vitro fertilization) and artificial insemination, can be, in Laura's words, "a nightmare, physically, emotionally, and spiritually; it was one attempt after another, one doctor to the next." Such treatments are costly, too. So is adoption. Laura estimates that adopting her Chinese daughter cost $28,000.

Finances are a particularly tough issue for single parents. Single midlife mothers of young children worry about how they will send their kids to college, not to mention save for retirement. My fifty-year-old friend laughs ruefully when she mentions that she'll be sixty-two when her six-year-old graduates from high school. "It helps that I'm a professional and from a middle-class family," says Annie. "It's a class privilege to go off and have a child on your own. I don't borrow money from my parents, but they pay for camp. As hard as it is, I know there's a cushion."

While all kids grow up with concerns, the children of these new families, like their mothers, are navigating virgin territory without maps. Dorothy's son, who at age five proudly announced that he had two mommies, has learned, now that he's fourteen, to be more circumspect. "In the third grade there was a fundamentalist kid who teased him and told him his parents would go to hell. Fortunately, his circle of friends rallied around him, and so did his teacher," recalls

Dorothy.

Annie, meanwhile, is coping with the matter of the anonymous donor. "The kids came home from school one day disturbed because their teacher said that everybody has a father, so their father must have died. I had to go in and tell the teacher, 'They don't have a father; they have a donor.' Now, I've learned my lesson and I march in at the beginning of every year to explain it all to the teacher."

Adoptive parents have different concerns, especially when their children come from other cultures. Laura, who is an observant Jew, wants to raise her daughter to be Jewish, yet she also wants to honor her Chinese culture and heritage. Fortunately, they live in Los Angeles, where there are many other families grappling with the same issues. Similarly, Dorothy and her partner don't feel isolated as lesbian parents. They live in New York City, where there is a supportive gay community. But outside of New York, Boston, Los Angeles, San Francisco, and a handful of other places, women in alternative families must make do with less support.

Still, children raised in alternative families have lives that are, in Annie's words, "ridiculously normal." And in key ways, they may have an advantage, growing up with mothers who are strong role models. As Dorothy points out, "Our son is growing up relying on both of us in a consistent way. He also sees that women can do everything."

shock treatment: becoming a mother

One thing that hasn't changed for our generation: Regardless of age or circumstances, becoming a mother is transformative. Childbirth itself is a miracle. "After the birth of my first child," says Noreen, the mother of two young adults, "I felt real reverence for my body. The fact that it could produce a child! I don't treat it shabbily anymore." Lola concurs. "Before I had a child it never occurred to me how amazing the world is. Now I think about how incredible it is to create another life, particularly a human life, and it's made me more appreciative of the natural world—flowers, animals, and plants. Having children made me see the world in a new way."

When we adopt, motherhood comes on quite suddenly, without the emotional preparation of pregnancy and childbirth. For Laura, the experience was frightening. "I wish I could say it was more thrilling. But the terror . . . We were sitting in the hotel lobby in China and this caregiver walked in with a tiny frightened baby and said, 'Here's your daughter.' It was instant immersion."

And motherhood? Many women I interviewed spoke with awe of the experience, using words like "huge," "amazing," "stunning," and "humbling" to capture its enormity. Joanne, mother of two daughters, thirty and eighteen years old, says, "My feelings for my kids are so powerful, they're scary. I've never comprehended the depth of love that one can feel for one's children. As much as you have enduring love for your partner, this is another kind of love. It's terrifying and so beautiful." Marion, who has two adolescents, a son and a daughter, agrees. "It's different from anything else, this sense that I would kill for my kids, do anything for them. It's a gift watching them grow and develop, and also receiving that kind of love from them." And Elizabeth, mother of two college-age sons, sums it up best: "It's the only thing I'm not ambivalent about in my entire life."

Studies also show that the role of mother is more central to women than the role of father is to men. In part, this is because, as psychologist Carol Gilligan, Ph.D., psychiatrist Jean Baker Miller, M.D., and others have theorized, women define themselves in relationship to others. Traditionally, boys have been raised with an emphasis on developing autonomy and an independent identity, preparing them for the world of work and public life. Meanwhile, as Dr. Miller writes in *Towards a New Psychology of Women*, " . . . women stay with, build on, and develop in a context of connections with others. Indeed, women's sense of self becomes very much organized around being able to make and then to maintain affiliations and relationships."

This certainly rings true for me. A year before our breakup, my husband and I strolled a sandy beach in San Francisco, talking about the impending changes in our lives as our children approached adulthood. He looked forward to it wholeheartedly. For him, the kids moving on meant freedom, plain and simple. Although he had always been seriously involved as a father—he'd been a stay-at-home-dad for years while I worked out of the house—he defined himself primarily by his work. It was different for me. I had been a working mom, with only short breaks for maternity leaves, and I had had a successful career in public health and freelance writing. But my career was a suit of clothes I put on every day; my family was who I was.

Defining ourselves through relationships, however, makes us more vulnerable to emotional conflict. For example, in a study conducted by child and family researcher Susan Silverberg, Ph.D., of 129 couples with children between ages ten and fifteen, mothers, but not fathers, were adversely affected by the disagreements they had with their youngsters regarding curfew, chores, free time, clothing choices, and other day-to-day issues.

Having children ups the ante for conflict in other ways, too. They can provoke enormous tension and trouble, even in long-term marriages. Laura and her husband had been together for fourteen years before they adopted their daughter. Their marriage had been stable and harmonious, but now they worry over money, don't have time for each other, and are too exhausted to have sex. "I had naïvely believed that we were going to share child care, and I think he believed that, too," she says. "That hasn't happened at all. I keep asking him, 'Why am I in charge? She's your daughter, too.'"

Not only do we suffer when we are at odds with our partners or our children, but we also have a hard time when they disagree with each other. In *Women of a Certain Age*, author Lillian B. Rubin, Ph.D., bears this out: "Over and over women tell of being . . . the interpreter between father and children, the buffer, the mediator, the one whose task it is to explain each to the other." Feeling this burden is part of being female in our culture, according to Demie Kurz, Ph.D., a sociologist at the University of Pennsylvania in Philadelphia. "As a girl, you're raised to be responsible for people's feelings and emotions. Women notice if someone is hurting because it's their job to notice."

As any parent knows, having children carries a host of day-to-day responsibilities, chores, and conflicts, or what writer Lionel Tiger has described as a "set of radically unselfish and often incomprehensibly inconvenient activities." Amanda, the mother of an adolescent son and daughter, adds, "Whether you like it or not, it's almost irrelevant. Being a mother changes you because it changes what you have to do, and what you're accountable for every day, regardless of how you feel."

Women usually feel the daily strain of having children around the house more intensely than do men. For example, in one study of more than 2,200 people, women living with children experienced more agitation than men, while men with children in the home experienced more satisfaction and emotional well-being.

We feel more burdened for good reason. Although fathers are taking on more household chores and helping more with child rearing, mothers still carry primary responsibility for these tasks, even if we work. Nor has the amount of time we spend in child rearing decreased as we have entered the workforce in large numbers. According to Ann Crittenden in *The Price of Motherhood*, "Researchers have confirmed . . . that the number of hours spent on primary care (that is, feeding, bathing, etc.) per child by white, married mothers in the United States almost doubled between the 1920s and the 1980s, a period in which the improvements in women's education and opportunities were nothing short of revolutionary."

In addition, although we have fewer children, there's more investment in each one. Ms. Crittenden writes, "Mothers in 1985 spent more *overall* time on child care than did mothers in 1920." There's also been a shift from "quantity to quality" in child rearing. At least as much, if not more, than our mothers, we perform time-consuming tasks, such as reading to our children and helping with homework. (I've always dreaded the words "I've got a project.") The bottom line is, we take our jobs as mothers very seriously.

our mothers, ourselves . . . not

Indeed, from stay-at-home mom to high-power professional, we've set the bar for ourselves as mothers very high. Our standards are often defined in opposition to the ways in which we ourselves were raised. Lynette grew up in a strongly matriarchal home. After going to college and studying child development, she decided to raise her daughter differently. "My mother couldn't understand why I'd ask my daughter, 'Do you want to do this, or that?' For her, it was 'Do what I tell you.' But I wanted to be an authority, not an authoritarian. So my daughter and I negotiated and talked about things."

In raising our children, we value and practice openness more than our parents did. "I've been much more open with my kids than my parents ever were; there were lots of subjects we never talked about," says Noreen, who grew up in a Catholic, Irish-American family. The payoff is that she's closer to her kids than she ever was with her parents.

Annie is likewise determined to be forthright with her children. When she was ten, her father died suddenly. "He had had several heart attacks, and nobody even told me he was sick. Two days after the funeral, my mother sent me to summer camp for eight weeks because she was collapsing. For years, I couldn't talk about my father without crying." So, when her children were seven years old and her sister became terminally ill, Annie was very straightforward. "I told them there was something wrong with her, and that she was going to die. You have to prepare kids for things like that."

When we are successful with our children, we benefit, too. Not only do we feel satisfied with a job well done, but we may also work out some of our own issues still unresolved since childhood. We can't relive our own childhoods, but we can heal old wounds by making sure that we don't repeat the mistakes that were made with us with our own children.

Sometimes, however, we overcompensate for our own mothers' failings. Bonnie admits she "smothered" her son. "I've always been a little obsessive, doing too much for him. My mother was well-meaning but pretty neglectful and self-absorbed. I think she was depressed and just not available. So my style of parenting was to do the opposite." Now, she struggles to help her son, age twenty, become less dependent.

It all comes down to balance. We struggle with the balance between career and family (more about that in chapter 6), and we also try to be good mothers without sacrificing ourselves.

trials and teenagers

It's tough enough to parent teenagers if you're in your late thirties or forties. It can be another experience entirely when you're in your fifties. We're already dealing with aging parents, outplacement at work, and hints of declining health. We're worrying about our appearance and our sexuality, and whether we're ever going to be able to retire. The cherry on the top? Our adolescent children, who remind us every day that we are, indeed, aging. As we glimpse their fleeting moments of maturity and notice them physically changing into adults, we realize we're also passing into another phase of life. Sometimes the reminder is more concrete. A friend of mine didn't know whether to laugh or cry when he repeated this comment from his teenage daughter: "Dad, you've already had your life."

When worries about appropriate supervision loom large, many of us make accommodation at work (like we've been doing for years already). When her children were teenagers, Ruth, who lived in a wealthy suburb, quit her job. "There was a lot going on in their lives that I was very concerned about. Suddenly, I had these adolescents and preadolescents who were getting into drinking and unsupervised parties. I was very concerned about who they were associating with. I realized that somebody had to be home." As in most couples, her husband was the primary breadwinner, so there was no question about who would stop working.

Single women often have a rougher time of it. Stephanie, a divorced mother, couldn't leave her job. But she was lucky, she says. "I have an incredibly flexible job. If my kid got sick I didn't go to work. And when my daughter was a teenager and I wanted to be around, I chose to work at home." Bonnie, also divorced, compromised on salary for a job that was around the block from her house. "The fact that I wasn't making much money was not the main point. I had a job I liked, and I could be there for my kid. He could stop in on his way home, or I could dash home to start dinner."

Raising teenagers can be especially complicated for midlife women. Studies have shown that mothers have both more intimacy and more conflict with their children at this time of life. But that's a double-edged sword; because while we are likely to communicate better with our teenagers, we, as opposed to our husbands, also remain their primary caretakers.

Certainly, the burden of daily child rearing chores diminishes as kids grow older. At the same time, we have to muster all of our skills of persuasion, reasoning, and negotiation. And when you have a daughter who'll argue to the death, as I do—my teenage daughter Emma's family nickname is Clarence Darrow—it's exhausting.

Fifty-something mothers of teenagers can't rely on the rules or standards our parents used. Cases in point: How much time were you allowed to spend on the Internet? What did your mother tell you about date-rape drugs? Nor do most of us have a lot of time to talk and share experiences with other mothers of teenagers. "There are no community norms and not a lot of sharing," offers Dr. Kurz of the University of Pennsylvania. "Everyone is so busy that they're just doing it on the fly."

With no obvious rules, we grapple with tough questions and are challenged by sophisticated teenagers. In response, we spend a lot of time worrying. If we have girls, we may fret more about rape and pregnancy, while mothers of boys tend to stew about physical violence and accidents—and everyone's anxious about our children getting into college—but we all do worry. It's as if we have a monopoly on anxiety.

I wasn't entirely surprised when Dr. Kurz, who studies women raising teenagers and is herself a mother, said, "Mothers in particular are carrying a huge amount of fear. We're afraid about everything. Partly it's because we live in what's been called a 'culture of fear.' But there's more going on. The health of youth is better than it has been, and teen pregnancy is down. Still, even when we hear reassuring statistics, we can't forget the fearful ones because we're ultimately held responsible." So responsible that, like Lynette, we may assume that people see our children as reflections of ourselves, not as separate individuals. "When my daughter was a teenager, I'd feel like a piece of me was there when she went out, and I wanted to make sure I was well represented."

Unfortunately, gender stereotypes don't go away. Like viruses, they have an uncanny ability to mutate to fit the circumstances. Mothers used to be blamed for everything from autism to mental illness to juvenile delinquency. (Remember *Portnoy's Complaint*?) "Now," says Dr. Kurz, "we have the updated stereotype of the bad mother—the career mother. A real mother would stay at home. Actually, it's even more ridiculous than that. We blame professional and working mothers for not being home, and welfare mothers for wanting to be home." Betty

Frain, Ph.D., a family therapist in Santa Barbara, California, and author of *Becoming a Wise Parent for Your Grown Child*, put it best: "Dr. Freud's been gone for a long time, but mother blaming is alive and well."

dealing with our daughters

There's a special twist for fifty-something women with teenage daughters. For example, some research has shown that as their daughters go through puberty, women report more intense midlife identity concerns and lower self-esteem. Seeing a daughter grow into an independent young woman can trigger a jumble of conflicting emotions. Just as we feel our own time is running out and our choices are narrowing, our daughters are taxiing for takeoff, full of plans for a bright, long future.

In addition, although many of us have careers, we were raised to be wives and mothers first. Our daughters are the first generation of women encouraged from birth to reach for the sky. We may have been brave enough to spend a junior year in Italy, but our daughters go off on wondrous (and scary) adventures to Vietnam, Nicaragua, and Africa. Despite our pride in their accomplishments and ambitions, we also may be envious and regretful of our own roads not taken. As Nancy Friday put it in *My Mother/My Self*, "Can you talk about the promise of womanhood, a career, motherhood—and not want a bit of that promise again if you yourself feel stifled?"

A year or so after my husband left, I was chatting with Emma one evening while I made dinner. She was groaning after a bad day, "These are supposed to be the best years of my life and I'm so miserable!" I quickly corrected her, pointing out that no one I knew (or in her right mind) would ever say that high school was the high point of her life. But I felt a wrench as I spoke. She had so many years ahead of her that might be her best, and I was afraid that mine were over.

We also confront another very here-and-now matter. Emma and I joke about our "dueling hormones," even though it isn't always amusing. Researchers suggest that during periods of reproductive changes, like puberty and menopause, we are especially vulnerable to stress, which affects us both mentally and physically. There's also, they say, "increased emotionality." No surprise there. Take one "PMS-ing" teenager, add one perimenopausal mother, and you may have a recipe for an emotional roller coaster, or an explosive week of laughing, crying, door slamming, and general storming around. Says Annie of her daughter, "She's become a raging adolescent. I don't know her anymore. She was so sweet, and now she's so awful. I miss her."

It's not just the hormones that get to us, though. It's the meaning behind those hormones. A daughter's first boyfriend can be a trigger for anxiety. Sue is a nurse-midwife who has spent her professional life helping women deal with issues of sexuality, birth control, and pregnancy. Yet, when I asked her what was hardest about being a mother, she answered, "When my daughter became sexually active." Although Sue made sure her daughter was protected, she still worried.

In addition to worrying about our daughters, we may also envy the excitement of their new experiences, especially if our own sex life is less than earth-shattering. "When you first start," reminisces Joanne, "when you're eighteen, you think, 'Oh my God, to be living with him, we could have sex every night, or twice a day.' It's been twenty-eight years now; that's a long time. We've become more open and more comfortable with each other, but sometimes being more comfortable can be like lying down for a good nap."

And woe to the single or divorced middle-aged mother who may actually be having or contemplating sex. Recently, after perusing a Victoria's Secret catalog, I was forced, in my ignorance, to ask Emma what a "tanga" was. After deigning to give me a slightly scornful explanation, she added, "Mom, you can't buy tangas. They're about being sexy, and you're not supposed to be sexy." (For the record, a tanga is a combination bikini-thong, worn to avoid panty lines.)

Besides hormones and sexuality, other parallel issues may cause tension for us and our girls. Like our daughters, who are trying to forge separate identities, we may be seeking more autonomy and a new way to define ourselves. As we anticipate the empty nest, we may contemplate going back to school, reentering the workforce, taking a promotion, or changing our careers. Noreen entered graduate school at the same time that her daughter, Beth, started college and her son, Tim, went to high school. "We all applied at the same time. I knew when Beth went away that I needed something else. So I went after the doctorate."

But it's harder for us than it is for our daughters to ask, "What am I going to do with the rest of my life?" For them, it's expected; it's part of growing up. For middle-aged women, it's still a relatively new idea, so we don't always get the support we need. Noreen's husband was ambivalent, although he did come through. Her mother, however, was another story. "She could not understand why I got my master's. And when I told her I was getting my doctorate, she was totally floored; she couldn't understand why my children and my marriage weren't 'enough.'"

Meanwhile, our daughters may resent our new freedom. We're feeling that it's finally time for us; yet they want us to be around, even if they're never home. And, of course, we feel guilty if we're not available when they do want us. Some researchers characterize the ambivalent mother–adolescent daughter relationship as "holding on and letting go." Our teenage daughters typically seesaw between forays into intimacy and attempts at separation. One day during her senior year in high school, Emma told me, "I'm sick of you, Mom. I'm glad I'm going to

Dad's for the week." The next day, she called me from school, heartbroken because she didn't get the role she wanted in the school play, and asked, "Can you take the afternoon off and hang out with me?"

In addition, one way daughters separate or shape their identities is by setting themselves up against their mothers. Because we came of age in the late 1960s and 1970s with mothers in traditional roles, we may have had an easier time differentiating ourselves. We rejected dressing in pumps and shirtwaists, being housewives or stay-at-home moms. In contrast, many of our daughters grew up with mothers who are doctors, lawyers, businesswomen, or professors, so they may find it harder to be different. Joanne says of her independent younger daughter—who is a strict vegetarian, has experimented with her sexuality, and deferred going to college after high school: "She is always pushing the envelope. She has an extraordinary need to do everything, to sort of devour life." According to Dr. Rubin, in *Women of a Certain Age*, a great deal of "separation work" goes on during a child's senior year in high school.

And so it seems that just as a nine-month pregnancy makes us ready and even grateful to arrive at childbirth, by the time the empty nest looms, it doesn't seem like such a bad prospect.

TAKING STOCK AND MOVING FORWARD

∽ Do you have regrets about not having children? Is adoption a possibility? Are there other children in your life with whom you can get more involved? Nieces and nephews? Can you volunteer at a local school or family service agency?

∽ Are you raising a child alone? Do you get enough support? Consider joining Parents without Partners or other groups sponsored by churches, synagogues, or community agencies. Can you ask your friends or relatives to babysit or help out in other ways?

∽ Are you feeling stressed by the pressures of children, husband, and job? Can you make some time for yourself?

∽ Have you talked to your teenagers about your own childhood? Sit down with an old photo album or your high school yearbook. Do a family tree. You're sure to share a few laughs.

∽ Do you give your teenager an allowance to teach money management? A clothing allowance is another useful tool.

∽ Are you constantly nagging your teenagers about chores, homework, coming home late? Have you set clear limits?

∽ Are you close to your teenager? Do your know their friends, where they spend their time, how they feel about drugs? About sex?

hey, this nest is supposed to be empty

dealing with "grown" children

> *"I have never yet met a client or known a friend who said any-thing other than 'The last one is leaving home, thank God.' Un-like their husbands, who are not burdened by the conflict between family and career, women are finally free to work as late as they want, travel on the job, or take a promotion."*
>
> —Betty Carter, family therapist and author of *Love, Honor and Negotiate: Making Your Marriage Work*

RESEARCHERS HAVE KNOWN THIS SECRET for decades, but the news is slow to leak out: The empty nest syndrome is a myth. "Many women confront the 'empty nest' not with a sense of dismay but with a sense of relief," wrote the authors of *Four Stages of Life*, a now-classic book about adult development. As important as motherhood is to those of us with children, no matter how you look at it, studies show that having children at home is stressful, and that the empty nest is linked to enhanced psychological well-being.

It may be distressing when our children move out, especially for stay-at-home or single moms. But it's rarely a crisis, and if it is, it doesn't last long. "That September, when Sean went off to college, I remember two weeks of actually feeling physical pain in my chest, like I had a hole in my heart, and my fingertips felt numb," says Bonnie. "I felt really horrendous. But I quickly got used to all this space and time for myself. I actually feel a little guilty about it."

Indeed, it's an opportunity for us to focus on self-development and to reinvent ourselves. Myra, mother of two, is already thinking about what will happen when her younger child leaves a year from now. "I find it inconceivable—all the decisions we have made for twenty-plus years have been for our children, at least to a large degree, and to have some of those needs and restrictions lifted is both frightening and exciting."

During the years when she and her husband raised four children, Sarah worked part-time. Her career was clearly secondary. But as her youngest child got ready to go off to college, Sarah felt a shift. "I found myself cleaning, clearing away, making room for new things. I had a new sense of openness and opportunity. All those things I'd clip from newspapers—I must do this, I'd like to do that. Now there's time."

Sarah says that separating herself from what was going on with her children was always difficult. Now that her nest is empty, she feels a sense of release. "The physical distance is allowing me to develop more emotional distance, which was harder to do when they were right here. I'm finding that I'm just as close to them, but in a healthier way."

When the kids move out, we no longer know where they are or

how late they are staying out. It's frightening to realize we can no longer keep tabs on them, but it's also a relief to go to bed at night unburdened by waiting—awake or half asleep—for them to get home.

With the children gone, we're able to refocus our emotional energy on ourselves. This energy sometimes unearths long-buried issues. "There's no question that I started to crash when I no longer had responsibility for the kids," says Alice, who has spent the last five years in therapy, dealing with shattering memories of childhood sexual abuse. "Till then, they had been the guiding force in my life. I've read that that's the case with other women who've been abused, that they can hold it together for their own children. It has to do with the job being done; it certainly did for me." Despite the anguish of unlocking her memory over the last few years, Alice is glad it happened. She no longer suffers from the brutal, debilitating headaches that plagued her for decades, and her relationship with her family has changed.

changes in ourselves and our relationships

The empty nest is actually a twentieth-century phenomenon, a product of our longer life spans. The time that couples spend alone after their last child leaves home has lengthened dramatically since the early 1900s, when a spouse (usually the husband) typically died less than two years after the last child married. Until relatively recently, notes Ms. Carter, "there was no such thing as 'grow old along with me.'"

Back in 1975, the authors of *Four Stages of Life* wrote, "Both men and women at this life stage tended to look forward to the departure of children as an event which would improve marital relations." Since then, numerous studies have confirmed that contentment with marriage follows a U-shaped curve, which tends to coincide with child-rearing responsibilities. In an article published in *Marriage and Family Review*, for instance, sociologists Linda K. George, Ph.D., and Deborah T. Gold, Ph.D., reported, "After the birth of children and especially during children's teenage years, marital satisfaction tends to decrease until the departure of children from the parental home. After the 'launching stage,' marital satisfaction increases again."

Some marriages improve dramatically. "Things got better between us because a huge source of our conflict was around how he dealt with the kids, and that conflict is gone," says Elizabeth. "Also, even though he's a depressive man with a tendency to withdraw, he rose up to fill the vacuum. When the kids were home, he'd retreat. Now if we're home alone, he might say, 'Talk to me while I putter in the basement,' or 'Come with me to walk the dog.' He's more present. He even volunteered to go to a movie with me this weekend—a rare thing."

Life often becomes more tranquil after the children leave. The days are quieter and less complicated; there's less cooking, laundry, and other household chores. We're freer to move around and travel, and we have fewer financial responsibilities (or at least the hope of the latter). More important, there is finally, as sociologist Irwin Deutscher, Ph.D., pointed out in 1964, " . . . freedom to be one's self for the first time since the children came along; no longer do the parents need to lead the self-consciously restricted existence of models for their children."

what if they don't fly?

It all sounds great, doesn't it? Unfortunately, there's another myth about the empty nest: They don't always leave and when they do, they often come back. During 2000, as the economy started to decline, nearly 11 percent of twenty-five- and thirty-four year-olds were living with their parents; among those between twenty-five and twenty-nine, nearly 12 percent were living at home. A November 2001 survey by Monstertrak.com, an online consulting and job placement firm, showed that 60 percent of college students plan to move back home after graduation; more than 20 percent said they planned to remain there for more than a year.

If there is an empty nest crisis, then, it doesn't occur when our children leave home; it's when they don't leave home on time. "Women our age enthusiastically plunged into parenthood," says Lola, whose twenty-four-year-old daughter struggled to become independent, "but in our heads it was a clear twenty-one-year commitment, after which we expected that they would be adults and therefore be a) not needy, b) helpful, or c) in a more equal relationship with us. We are done with our part of the commitment, and they are not. Now, with the kids over twenty-one, we've depleted our resources, and we're resentful of not being free and creating a new, more adult relationship with them."

Those in blended families may feel this more acutely. It may be difficult to establish the lines of authority with stepchildren, and there may be resentment if they hang around too long. "As much as we love our children," says Maria Tupper, a clinical social worker in private practice, "there's a way in which a couple in a good relationship reunites when the kids leave. In a blended family, this can become a problem if one partner feels, 'I signed on to help out till she went to college. When do we ever get to be alone?'"

what if they come back?

In addition to children who don't leave home on schedule, we also now have "boomerang" kids, who move in and out when it's convenient or necessary. In the three years since my older daughter, Kate, graduated college, she's lived with me, rented her own apartment nearby, and then moved to New York City. She returned to Connecticut, moved back in with me, and then moved into an apartment with a roommate. Now, she is temporarily living in her father's house.

Her pattern is no anomaly. According to a study in the *Journal of Marriage and the Family* by William S. Aquilino, Ph.D., of young adults ages nineteen to thirty-four who had left home at least once, 42 percent had returned at some time, more than 10 percent more than once. When things go wrong—they lose a job, divorce, or break up with a partner—our children come home. They also return when they're "in between"; when they finish school or leave the armed forces, for example. According to research by Julie DaVanzo, Ph.D., senior economist at the RAND Corporation, and Frances Goldscheider, Ph.D., sociologist at Brown University, our home "is not only a 'safety net' for young adults who have run into unexpected twists on the road to independence, but also a 'home base' to return to while encountering many of the often frequent changes that occur at this stage of the life course." It's tough on us, and probably not particularly healthy for our children. Ms. Tupper feels that "in the long run, they don't feel so good about themselves."

What's happening? For one thing, adolescence has expanded at both ends. According to Stephen Small, Ph.D., a researcher who focuses on parenting and adolescence at the University of Wisconsin in Madison, "Adolescence has a physical beginning—puberty usually marks the start—and a social/emotional ending, which has to do with being financially independent, having a mature, intimate relationship, and having a degree of independence from the family of origin, at least moving out of the parents' house." Not only do the physical changes of puberty occur earlier than they used to, but it also takes longer for our children to become independent.

Before 1960, young adults got married and left home. Period. Usually, once they were gone, they were gone. Our children, however, stay in school longer and marry later. Today, the average age for a first marriage is twenty-six, four years older than it was in 1970. Assuming they do get married, of course. Since the 1970s, more and more young adults live together before marriage. In 1992, for example, there were 3.3 million unmarried couples living together in the United States, over six times the number in 1970. But these new living arrangements are fragile. According to the National Center for Health Statistics, the probability of a first marriage ending in separation or divorce within five years is 20 percent; for a couple living together, the likelihood of a breakup increases to 49 percent.

In addition, many single young adults leave home to live on their own. But that's harder to do now that jobs are more scarce, and graduate school is often necessary to launch a solid career. Housing costs have also skyrocketed. I graduated college in 1970 and moved to Boston. When I landed a job that paid $7,500 a year, I was able to pay all my expenses and save money. Today, many young adults can't make it without help; some of them are already saddled with student loans. In addition, our generation decamped particularly quickly. Three-quarters of the early baby boomers, born between 1948 and 1954, were gone from their parents' homes by age twenty-one. "The current generation of parents was the generation that left home earlier than any, before or since, to get married, to go to college," says Dr. Goldscheider. "It was also easier to maintain a single lifestyle then. The three decades since then have been very different and much has changed."

However, there are more than demographic and socioeconomic trends at play. Our kids aim very high, and they have different expectations than we did. Coming of age during the antiwar, civil rights, and women's movements, many of us rejected the materialistic values of our parents and American "bourgeois" society. "When I was a young adult, I lived in a really inexpensive house," says Betty Frain, Ph.D., a family therapist in Santa Barbara, California. "Everything we had was hand-me-down, and we loved it. We were proud of getting by and improvising. Now, kids expect things to be new. It's partly the culture—what they've been exposed to in advertising and movies. They expect to have it all immediately. Kids aren't glad to have junker cars, like we were."

Sound familiar? Women I talk to say that their twenty-something children expect to have the same material possessions as their fifty-something parents. They don't know they're *supposed* to be poor. In addition, some families are so wealthy, successful, or famous that the kids know they can't come close, which inhibits them from even trying to be on their own (or ever *needing* to be on their own).

What's more, parents and children today remain emotionally entwined longer than we did with our parents. According to an article by Tamar Lewin in the *New York Times* in January 2003, there has been "a fundamental rethinking of a child's departure for freshman year as the stark marker of separation and independence." Thanks to cell phones and e-mail, many parents are in near-constant contact with their kids. The article goes on to describe parents editing their children's papers, discussing their clothing choices, and helping them with roommate problems. They even stay the night in their children's dorm rooms.

This would have been unthinkable to us. Lola, who more often than she prefers finds herself being her daughter's confidant/therapist, agrees. "The big distinction is that our generation would never, ever, bar none, have talked to our parents in this way, unless it was something so severe we were forced to. Our friends were our sounding boards. By twenty-one I was emotionally autonomous and not my parents' child. Kids of this generation don't have the drive to autonomy that we had."

Our parenting styles may also have contributed to the boomerang phenomenon. "A lot of people tell me that when they were growing up, they never had a voice, and there was no way they'd go ever back home," says Demie Kurz, Ph.D., a sociologist at the University of Pennsylvania. "Today's parents are not generally permissive, but they maintained an atmosphere where the children were a little more equal. It's possible we've created environments that are easier to come back to."

living with adult children

When young adult children live at home, studies suggest that most of

the time, there's a great deal of positive interaction between parents and their twenty-something "roommates." However, there's also plenty of room for conflict. In one survey conducted by Dr. Aquilino, the majority of problems stemmed from helping around the house (58 percent) and money (39 percent).

When they're home, adult children often revert to teenage behaviors, and unfortunately, many of us allowed our teenagers to slack off. "A seven-year-old is thrilled to help, but we don't develop that sense," suggests Dr. Goldscheider. "Parents take over chores as their kids get older. Kids get out of chores by saying, 'I have a test tomorrow' or 'I have a game.' Parents accept those priorities because education has become so important."

Unless we force a change, that is. These days, Bonnie treats her twenty-year-old son differently when he's home on breaks from college. "It's a conscious decision. Before, I'd have done everything for him, without him even asking. Now I try to do only what he absolutely needs me to do. I'm trying to give him space because I think he's less mature than a lot of people his age. But he really doesn't like it. He tells me I've become a neglectful mother!"

Gender issues can, and do, come into play. In Dr. Goldscheider's research, "the guys get much more of a free ride. Parents are less disturbed when they leave dishes in the sink or a mess in the living room. They expect daughters to help with housework, or else the daughters simply see what needs to be done and they do it because of their early training."

Whether the boomerang kid is a son or daughter, experts say it's important to be clear about expectations from the outset. Dr. Kurz has had personal experience with a boomerang son. "When he moved back in, we laid down rules. You don't leave dishes out, you take out the garbage, you empty the dishwasher, and so forth. And we made it clear that we'd give the same rules to any adult who came to visit, so he didn't think we were being overly parental."

I've found that there are also personal issues. For example, should you know where your adult daughter is going and what time she'll be home? How can you avoid knowing more than you want to about her life, particularly with the opposite sex, just by virtue of living in close quarters? Obviously, when my daughter returned home after college, she was too old for a curfew. Still, I noticed when I woke up during the night and she wasn't home yet. Dr. Goldscheider suggests putting this concern right out on the table. "You can ask whether she wants you to call the police if she's not home by early morning."

money, money

Another big concern is finances. When grown children live at home, who pays for what? How do we foster financial self-sufficiency? Some of us throw up our hands. "Financially independent—ha-ha. What in the world is that?" laughs Ruth. We can establish guidelines, depending on our own needs and resources. Some middle-class parents charge rent and expenses. Others allow a temporary rent-free existence, as long as the child is saving money for a move to his or her own apartment.

And what about graduate school? Most of us agree that it's legitimate to pay for college. But afterward, how much money and for how long are big questions. That $30,000 no longer needed for tuition will go a long way toward fixing up a shabby kitchen or buying a piece of land in Vermont. Noreen says, "Our children don't have loans from college. But for graduate school, we want them to have some financial stake, so we insisted that our daughter take out a loan. Still, we're subsidizing her living expenses, and it's a big bite."

There's no right or wrong. What's key is figuring out the level of involvement, financial and otherwise, that is appropriate for us and our child. Are we crippling them or empowering them, and how do we know the difference? "You have to weigh that from day to day," says Dr. Frain. "How independent are they? If they're going to school, are they doing okay? Who are they hanging out with? What kinds of jobs are they getting? Are they making decisions? Do they have goals? If your kid says he's an artist or a writer but he doesn't write or produce anything, there may be a problem."

When a twenty-something child moves back home, it's important to set objectives and establish how long he's planning to stay. Maybe he lost a job or broke up with a girlfriend and he just needs time to lick his wounds. Perhaps he wants to save money for a short period. Talking about it helps clarify whether there's another, unexpressed agenda. For example, a daughter who moves back after her parents' divorce may be doing it to take care of her newly single mom.

The clearer we can be, the better. Dr. Frain advises her clients to put it all in writing. "I suggest something like this: 'We love you and are glad to help. But this is our house, and we call the shots, so this is what we expect and what we have to offer. You can take six months and pay this amount of rent. We will put part of it into savings for you. We expect you to cook once a week and do the food shopping.' You can negotiate back and forth, but do put it on paper. Then bring it out in three months, look at it, and update it if necessary."

In addition, it may be time to revise our ideas about what's normal. According to Dr. Aquilino's research, parents with two or more children are more likely than not to have at least one adult child return home. Of the returnees, 90 percent stayed less than four years, and two-thirds left before two years had passed. He described these stays as "relatively short," although some of us might quibble with that description. Still, considering my own experience, I find it reassuring that Dr. Aquilino writes, "Home leaving is best construed as a process of separation for many children."

after they're launched

The landscape of parenthood changes once our children finally move out for good. Of course, as parents, we're always on call. But as the daily intensity recedes, we face the new challenge of developing a more equal, adult relationship.

Many of our twenty-something children remain dependent on us financially. Parents often continue to provide money or loans for some time. It's still hard to know how much to subsidize our kids. We may choose to spend the money in order to get them out and living on their own so we can reclaim our privacy. On the other hand, this may conflict with their need to be independent. How do we strike a comfortable balance? Of her twenty-four-year-old daughter, Lola says, "I want her to be rich enough not to starve, but poor enough to have to struggle."

Regardless of where they live, emotional boundaries are still an issue. Our goal is for our children to be independent but emotionally connected. We want to set the stage so that we can make the transition from parent to friend.

Sure, there are things that parents and children can't and shouldn't tell each other. When I started dating, it was clear that my daughters wanted minimal information, and there were certainly issues that I would talk about only with friends, not with them; likewise, there are also things I don't want to know. However, when adult children are older, such intimate conversations can be helpful to both.

Even though you're always a parent, you can slowly become more of a peer. Joanne describes her relationship with her younger daughter: "We have pretty open discussions about values, politics, goals, gender, sexuality, all those things. I no longer feel that I have to hold myself back as a mother. I can be clear about who and what I am."

It takes a conscious effort to make the transition. Says Dr. Kurz, "Part of the struggle of becoming a friend to your kid and breaking down the parental role is convincing him you're not going to treat him like a child. It's not easy. You've got to keep your mouth shut sometimes. Or you have to try not to sound like a parent. Sometimes my kids say, 'That was helpful, but you can't talk that way to me anymore.'" Women are often more successful in making this switch. Dr. Kurz continues, "Women are better at framing things; we have indirect ways of making suggestions. Instead of saying, 'Look, do it this way,' we might say, 'Oh, have you thought of this?'"

Dramatic life events can also nudge mothers into new perceptions and more adult relationships. Louisa, whose son is married and just became a father, says, "Now I can finally see him as an adult man."

When one of our parents dies, we often become closer to our adult children. "Older kids, even beginning as young as sixteen or seventeen, recognize that it's tough for a parent to lose a parent," says Debra Umberson, Ph.D., a sociologist at the University of Texas. "It's also a shared loss, because they're losing a grandparent. They tend to be more supportive; they help out more. It's a positive trigger for change in relationships with older kids. For parents, it's the first glimmer of role reversal, seeing how their kids will take care of them. You look at your kids in a different way."

A similar change happened when my marriage fell apart. In the weeks after my husband left, my daughter Kate, who was away at college, called or e-mailed me every day. She sent flowers with a note saying, "Don't forget, we're in this together," and another card saying, "Not a day goes by that I'm not thinking of you." She, of course, was hurting, too. But in our mutual pain, we forged a new, more adult relationship.

The transition to a more adult relationship becomes more difficult if your child has health problems. For example, Joanne's thirty-year-old daughter, Amy, has a chronic inflammatory disease. "Amy is careful how much she tells me about her illness. Until I can stop being so worried, I'm acting like her mother and not a peer." Amy and her boyfriend moved across country several years ago, and when she needed surgery, Joanne faced a major conflict. "I wanted to fly out there and take charge, but I knew I had to let them deal with it themselves," she says. She resolved it by flying out after the surgery, when she could cook or be helpful around the house. "It was a good compromise. I was able to do something worthwhile, instead of hover and worry and be useless."

If we're lucky, most parent-child relationships will span more than fifty years. Even if we don't become close friends, our relationships do become more equal and mature. Sometimes, things don't work out and we're disappointed. Says Louisa of her son and daughter-in-law, "It's not like they're doing anything horrible. But I would never have picked Janet for him to marry. They're just kind of conventional. We don't have much in common." Or as Sue Berlin, a divorced middle-aged teacher who is estranged from her grown daughter, says in the movie *Judy Berlin*: "I imagined the two of us sitting at a concert or discussing something from *The New Yorker*. An educator and her daughter," she says, laughing. "I thought we would be such good friends. Well, I still get *The New Yorker*."

When does the job of active mothering end? I'm convinced that being a mother goes on forever, but as an old friend and long-time pediatrician always reminds me, "All children do grow up eventually." For many of us, how we mother changes significantly during our fifties, when we launch our nearly grown children, and it becomes time to mother ourselves.

Taking Stock and Moving Forward

∞ If you feel bereft when your children leave home, take advantage of your newfound freedom with classes, cooking for friends, a book group to fill the void. And remember, they'll be back!

∞ Is your child still living at home? Is it because it's easy and comfortable? Or because she can't afford to live on her own? When your child is ready (or when you are!), work with her to develop a plan for an independent living situation. Can you afford to subsidize the rent or another expense to enable her to move out?

∾ Can you find ways to encourage your boomerang child's independence? Have him cook dinner a couple of times a week? Do the laundry? Address the realities of what life costs. Can you charge your child rent and ask him to buy some groceries and pay for his own phone line and car insurance?

∾ If you have a grown child who is out of the home, are there ways that you can foster closeness and a more peerlike relationship? Perhaps a yearly vacation together? A subscription to a series of plays? A monthly facial? A weekly dinner and a movie? Monitor yourself: Are you still in your parenting role, or are you having the kind of conversations you would have with a friend? This shift is important for both of you.

∾ Do you and your grown child living away have different expectations of how often you should communicate? You may think you're supporting her privacy, and she may think you've abandoned her (and vice versa)! Ask how often she'd like to hear from you.

climbing and jumping off the career ladder

professional concerns

> *"I've been asked a number of times, 'How did you succeed so quickly?'" she once said. "The answer is I was middle-aged, had varicose veins and I didn't have time to fool around."*
>
> —The *New York Times* obituary for Mary Kay Ash, founder of Mary Kay Cosmetics, November 14, 2001

WHEN TRISH REACHED FIFTY, it was a turning point. "It's freed me," she says. "I see it as the final release. I have permission now to accept that I've had a great career, and I'm not striving to go further." The CEO of a small publishing firm, she's where she wants to be, and she also knows what got her there. "I'm articulate and responsive, and I make decisions; I don't waffle. I work fast, I get a lot done, and I make money for the company." Put simply, she's at the top of her game.

Other fifty-something women feel more empowered to express themselves at work. Says Jill, a partner in a "boutique" public relations firm, "Your judgments become much clearer. I no longer suffer fools. I've become more selective as I age. I find myself in meetings saying, 'No, that idea's not going to work.' I just blurt it right out. I only have so much time. I also pick and choose my clients so that I don't get saddled with time wasters and nitpickers. And I charge a little more than my competition. I'm worth it, and my clients know it."

Like Trish and Jill, many of us find that after years of effort, we've arrived at positions of power in our organizations; we can finally take part in meaningful decision making and fulfill our talents. Some of us go back to work after a divorce or years of working part-time in order to raise children. Thwarted ambitions, bias, or hitting the glass ceiling may impel us to begin new careers. Whatever our situation, this is a time of life when we ask what our work means to us and how it can be more fulfilling.

Until two years ago, Christine was one of a handful of women partners in a large, prestigious law firm. She was also one of the most highly respected female lawyers in her state. But she left her job to start her own practice, taking a considerable drop in income. Why? "One evening at a company retreat, one of the other women partners had a little too much to drink. The men were joking at her expense and making snide comments. Something clicked, and I realized that I'd never be completely comfortable with them, and what's more, I didn't want to be."

Like many other fifty-something women, Christine had set out to make her way in a man's world. She thought she'd have it all—the perfect career in law, a high income, and a wonderful family. To succeed, though, she had had to adapt to a male career model. It was all right for a long time. But during her fifties, when many of us question where we are and where we're going, she decided she no longer wanted to compromise with the male culture at her job. She realized she had the skills and contacts to hang out her own shingle. So she walked away.

little miss homemaker?

Women of our generation were not necessarily led to think that we'd have careers. For the most part, our mothers didn't. Even if they'd worked before we were born, many became homemakers after they had children. "My mother ran three factories during the war," says Noreen. "But when my father was furloughed he said they couldn't both work, so she went home and stayed with the kids. She had a lot of abilities, but she really was a 1950s mom."

Nor was college a foregone conclusion for our mothers. Ruth's mother was a "very smart woman who never had any support at home as far as getting an education. After high school she was sent to finishing school in Switzerland." Similarly, although Natalie's mother wanted to be a teacher, she worked as a teacher's aide. Natalie explains, "It was her brother who got to go to college."

Often, even college-educated women didn't work outside of the home. Some got involved in volunteer work. Alice's mother, for example, graduated from a "Seven Sisters" college and became a highly visible, unsalaried political appointee in her state. Bonnie's mother was an economics major at an Ivy League university. "She dropped out of a master's of economics program, got married, and never worked," Bonnie says. "If she had had some encouragement and didn't have embedded in her brain the idea that only men know what they're doing, she probably would have become an economist and been less angry, not so horrible to be around. I think she was really disappointed and depressed my whole life. She slept every afternoon. Today, I think, 'Who sleeps every afternoon?'"

Even when our mothers were educated working women, their jobs tended to be secondary. Marsha's mother worked with her husband every day. "But it always felt like she was a homemaker who was helping out, not that she had career goals of her own." It was not until the mid-sixties, with the emergence of the feminist movement, that women began going back to school and seeking jobs in greater numbers.

For most of us, even if we planned to work, our vision was narrowly focused. We were encouraged to do well in school and to go to college, but there was a hidden—or perhaps not so hidden—agenda. Diane Tickton Shuster writes in *Women's Lives through Time*, "During this postwar, prefeminism period, middle-class girls received mixed messages about the value of their education: Going to college was considered highly desirable, but, for many, earning the 'Mrs.' degree was more important than acquiring marketable skills for the workplace." Trish adds, "When I was a young woman in the late 1970s, I expected to work, but I was not burdened with particularly challenging goals to achieve, because just working was an accomplishment. Nowadays, women in their twenties and thirties are supposed to be vice presidents in no time at all."

I never thought about a "career" when I was growing up in the 1950s. (I'm happy to say this is in stark contrast to how my daughters think about their lives.) My parents always said, "Be a teacher. It's something you can go back to after your children are grown." Millions of girls received that same message, or something close. Alice, who became a lawyer, recalls, "It was conveyed by word that women were supposed to have a career. For me, it was, 'You should be a teacher or a nurse,' even though my mother thought she was the most enlightened lady on the face of the earth. So I got a master's in teaching at Columbia—a total waste." Again and again in my interviews, I heard the same story, regardless of where we grew up. "For girls in the sixties in Barbados," says Lynette, "it was either nursing or teaching, especially if you were from a poor background. Of all the people I knew, I was the first to go to college."

There were exceptions, of course. Jill, one of three girls in her family, says, "The mantra from both parents was, 'You can do or be whatever you want.' My father wouldn't allow us to take typing in high school, even though all my friends did. He wanted to make sure we didn't end up as secretaries." Lola, a school administrator, adds, "It was the same for my brother and me. They didn't raise either of us to have particular careers, but they were very clear that we should be independent." Still, her mother told her, "You need to be able to have choices in case you don't marry." It's unlikely she said that to her son.

blazing a new trail

In 1945, on the eve of the baby boom, a *Fortune* magazine poll showed that 63 percent of Americans thought a woman should not work if her husband could support her. Women just a bit older than us didn't have the support of their husbands, either. A friend of mine, now in her early seventies, tells me that when she was in her forties, she told her husband she wanted to apply for a position at a nearby private school. He told her it was all right with him, but "only one of us is allowed to be tired, and it's not you."

Today, six in ten women work (the comparable figure for men is seven in ten), and the dual-career family is the norm. When our children watch reruns of *Leave It to Beaver*, June Cleaver, cleaning house in her pumps and pearls, may as well be a Martian.

We've lived through a social and political revolution. According to Hilarie Lieb, Ph.D., who teaches economics at Northwestern University, there was a defensive flurry of educational reform in response to the Russians' launch of Sputnik in 1957. "Among baby boomers, there was a jump in people who graduated high school and received BAs, and it was greater for women than for men. Once women were better educated, it changed their whole decision-making process. They wanted to use their education."

But probably much more important was the emerging women's movement. Sparked by Betty Friedan's bombshell, *The Feminine Mystique*, published in 1963, in which she attacked the status quo and inspired us to get out there and fight for equality, we shared an awakening with millions of our "sisters."

At the same time, we were caught up in other changes. Rising divorce rates were an eye-opener: We couldn't count forever on husbands for economic security. The economic woes of the 1970s, the globalization of the economy, and growing insecurity for many American workers forced families to rely on two incomes to keep up their standards of living. By 1997, according to a *Fortune* article, in 84 percent of married couples, both partners worked.

between a rock and a hard place

Our daughters think of career as a given. But we are the transitional generation. Raised conventionally, we decided midstream that career really did matter. We've had to bushwhack as we go. In the series of studies of the Radcliffe class of 1969, by definition a group of high-achieving women, the researcher reported, "Many have had to make decisions without much precedent or fight new and old stereotypes to live the lives they felt were best for themselves and/or their families."

Fired up and eager to enter the working world, many of us confronted mind-numbing sexism. Lola recalls job hunting in 1970:

"People kept asking me how many words a minute I typed. So I finally said to this guy, 'I graduated from a very respectable college, and if I were a man you would never ask me how many words a minute I typed.' And he said, 'But you're not a man, and this is the Midwest.'" She didn't get the job. Being in the Midwest, however, was apparently not the problem. When Alice met with the dean of admissions at a top Eastern law school, he told her to "go back to the dishwasher." She didn't give up; instead, she went to the University of Chicago.

Even if we escaped such obvious prejudice, we faced other, more subtle discrimination. In many professions, women were funneled into "feminine" pigeonholes. Young female doctors went into pediatrics; a study done as late as 1985 reported that women who chose surgery or other male-dominated specialties faced harassment and hostility.

Similar sifting went on in the law. After spending a year working on a high-profile murder case, Alice joined a law firm and was promptly assigned to family law. "It happened to many women lawyers. They thought that they needed women to do it because divorce is very personal; women were better listeners, and they'd be more empathetic." Annie bucked the trend and became a criminal lawyer, but her career has not been without problems. She says, "It's very hard for women who are criminal defense lawyers in private practice. People think a man will do a better job, be more aggressive."

Once on the job, then, we had to deal with sexual innuendo. Men, unused to women in the workplace in peer positions, tended to treat us as sweet young things or sexual objects. Joanne recalls, "I was assigned a black male assistant who seemed to have a need to show that I was 'just a woman.' One day as I was leaning over his desk to point out something, he grabbed me and kissed me. I reported him for sexual harassment."

Lynette, an educational policy consultant, struggled with both sexism and racism in a state bureaucracy. "I lived in Canada more than twelve years and never experienced the type of racism I experienced here. The first few years, I was the new kid on the block, and I had thirteen districts to monitor while others had five. I thought it was because I was a woman, and maybe because I'm black. I still get it; even with a Ph.D., it doesn't matter."

However, in some cases being female was an advantage. Trish, the publishing CEO, explains, "I think being a career woman at that time was surprising, and it did help me. It established me immediately as distinctive and gave me much more visibility."

our own worst enemies

In addition to institutionalized bias, we've struggled with our own bogeymen. Some of us have the "imposter syndrome," or what Carol McIntosh, Ph.D., of the Wellesley Centers for Women in Massachusetts, calls "feeling like a fraud." It's "the feeling that in taking part in public life one has pulled the wool over others' eyes; that one is in the wrong place, and about to be found out; that there has been a colossal mistake in the selection and accreditation process which the rest of the world is about to discover." Not only do we feel undeserving or out of place but also, just like Groucho Marx, who famously quipped, "I don't care to belong to a club that accepts people like me as members," we think that anyone who believes we are talented or competent must be stupid.

Louisa manages an art therapy program, but it took her a while to feel legitimate in her job. "I was always feeling that I was sort of faking it and that I got a job I'm not qualified for. But it has worked out; it's just enough power so that I feel comfortable." Imposter issues are especially prevalent among academic women, where reactions like

Myra's, when she was offered a tenured faculty position at a prestigious Midwestern college, are not unusual: "I can't believe they want *me*. I feel like I have to go out and read everything there is in the field so I'll know what I'm doing."

If we have children, we face other internal demons. Fresh from the barricades, we assumed we could have it all. But we were blindsided by how difficult it has actually been to balance our roles as wives, mothers, and workers. Caught between the competing demands of work and family, we leaned toward family, yet it was hard to find a comfortable choice. After she left her law firm when her adopted children were adolescents, Ruth recalls, "I felt that I didn't have much to say anymore. At a party, when somebody would ask me what I did, it was hard, really hard. I'd say, 'Well, I take care of the kids and I do community work.' I was embarrassed."

Those of us who did work felt a sharp wrench between home and job. As novelist Elizabeth Berg wrote in *The Pull of the Moon*, "We flowered in the sixties, but the spirit of the fifties was deep in us." When her younger daughter was a toddler, Joanne, an urban planner, turned down a position she desperately wanted. "I could have contributed something nationally, had a real presence and more of an effect on issues important to me. It would have meant a long commute, a lot of travel, days and maybe even weeks away from home. Did I really want to be that kind of person? I had made the decision to have children, and I didn't want to do that to them or to me. It was an agonizing choice, but it's not a decision I regret."

More often than not, our misgivings came when we did put career before family. "Full-time was really hard," says Sue, "especially being a midwife and being on call. I do have some regrets. I always missed Billy's square dances at school. When I look back at the pictures, I wonder, was it really worth it for me to be catching somebody else's baby?" Amanda, who until recently was a corporate executive, describes one of her dilemmas: "I had just gotten a promotion, and an important meeting was scheduled. I'll never forget leaving my son, who was sitting on the couch burning up with fever, with the babysitter while I dashed downtown to the conference room."

We have problems that men just don't have. We don't, or can't, compartmentalize as efficiently as men do because our boundaries between work and home are more permeable. If things aren't going well at home, we don't feel successful at work, either. Guilt is our constant companion.

Ironically, feminism, which has done so much for us, has also indirectly contributed to our guilt. Deborah Carr, Ph.D., an assistant professor of sociology at Rutgers University, points out, "Baby boom women wanted to live up to the ideals set by the women's movement. They may feel bad about themselves for not achieving."

Our mistake, says Dr. Carr, is that we tend to blame ourselves. Full-time work causes difficulties, not because we are conflicted or inadequate, but because of social and economic realities—the lack of affordable, high-quality child care, the absence of paid family leave or other support on the job, the fact that we still do more of the housework. "The structural support just isn't there," says Brown University sociologist Frances Goldscheider, Ph.D. "In this country, your child is like your cat, or some project you take on. It's your individual decision to have a child and your problem to take care of it." (As we get older, if we're caring for spouses or aging parents, it's like déjà vu.)

Whatever the problems, we did make different choices from our mothers when we had children. "Women now in their fifties did not exit the labor force altogether, then go back and take a job selling perfume at Macy's after the kids were gone," says Dr. Carr. "They have been working continuously, even if it was part-time or in their homes." Although we kept working, most of us interrupted or compromised our careers for our children, willingly or not. We took maternity leave or less pay for more flexible hours.

In general, women work fewer years than men. In 1998, the average sixty-two-year-old woman had worked for twenty-nine years; her male counterpart had worked for thirty-eight years. And this has cost us, personally and financially. Full-time female workers earn 77.5 cents for every dollar earned by men. Over an average lifetime, the cumulative earnings for a fifty-year-old woman are $496,000; for a fifty-year-old man, it's $1.1 million.

Some of this disparity is sexism. But that's not the whole story. By 1991, what Jane Waldfogel, Ph.D., professor of social work at Columbia University, calls the "family gap" in wages between mothers and nonmothers was larger than that between women and men. On average, mothers earn 10 to 15 percent less than nonmothers.

work matters

Of course, work is important to us for economic reasons. But it also develops our talents and contributes to our self-esteem and identity. A 1998 Catalyst survey of graduates of twelve top-ranked business schools reported, "Forty-one percent of women and 27 percent of men surveyed agree that women are less likely to be motivated by money."

In an in-depth study of fifteen women who left positions at Fortune 500 or 1000 companies, Jill Silverstein, Ph.D., an organizational development specialist, found, "Status and money weren't the main motivators in their daily work. It was getting zest and energy from the work they did, the reward of satisfying work, the opportunity to work collaboratively." Trish is a prime example. "I love the business and love to share it. I enjoy working with bright young people who want to learn. I like being older; I feel legitimate, genuinely experienced. I really do know something after thirty years, and I enjoy teaching it."

Furthermore, our jobs may provide a refuge from home. "I had a bunch of people who worked for me—I was the boss. I could tell people what to do and they did it!" says Amanda. "It was gratifying and much clearer than in other parts of my life, including my family. In part, it was a way of escaping the drudgery of motherhood." Work also helps us claim space for ourselves, like it does for Noreen, who teaches at a college. "I always needed to know I could take care of myself and to have something that was mine. My husband is a dominant personality, and I needed to not always be his wife or Beth and Tim's mom. When I stand in front of a class, I stand or fall on my own."

Career is especially important for women going through divorce, not only to provide a financial base but as structure for the day. It's also a welcome distraction and a boost for damaged self-esteem. I was worried because I had a huge deadline to meet one year after my husband left. It was hard to do, but as it turned out, it gave me a reason to get up every morning and a sense of pride when I finished on time.

Moreover, many women can't imagine their lives without work. "I needed work, for self-definition, for money and independence," says Joanne. "Besides, I enjoyed it. I'd have been bored to death all these years without working, doing something productive and feeling engaged."

Most of the women I interviewed expressed the need to help others or make an impact on the world through their jobs. Annie's work stems directly from her experiences as an activist in the 1960s and 1970s. "One of the reasons I started doing criminal law was because I wanted to be available and knowledgeable when people got arrested in demonstrations or because of their politics. Today, doing criminal defense is political in the sense that virtually everybody who is arrested is poor or minority. That doesn't mean that I'm behind people selling drugs, and it doesn't mean I'm doing something political every day. But the reason I'm in legal work is to achieve social justice."

The happiest women are those who, like Annie, have a sense of purpose. Stephanie, who is a researcher and advocate for progressive environmental policies, agrees. "I work because I like to work. I love nothing more than feeling like my mind is going full throttle. And I work because I believe in what I'm doing. I feel driven to be the person that says, 'This is what we need to do it better. The job isn't done.'"

time for a change

The job is far from done, not just out there in the world, but in our own lives. The women I interviewed have no intention of leaving work. On the contrary, like me, they are excited, ambitious, and full of ideas. Some of us have concrete plans, while others are still figuring out the path or allowing ourselves to dream. But everyone's focused optimistically on the future. Here are some of their voices:

- Erica, a writer: I'm just beginning. I think success will come in the next few years. I'd like to have some impact on the world through my work, to write a novel that has emotional impact, and I'd like a lot of people to read it.

- Lynette, an educational policy consultant: I'd like to start my own school and say that I'd contributed to some kids' lives. And I'd like to form an experimental housing co-op, with college students, women on welfare, professionals; a mixed community, black and white. I think if we live a certain way and have common goals, we can change people.

∽ Marion, a midwife: I want to figure out what I'm meant to be doing. I know I'm meant to be doing something; maybe it's exactly what I am doing. It's a journey.

∽ Noreen, a college instructor: I'd like to contribute to the world in a larger way. I'd like for my research in counseling to become known.

∽ Corinne, a school administrator: I come from a long-lived family, so I want to take care of my health and develop all those interests I can continue into old age: writing, playing the piano . . .

∽ Judith, the owner of a spa: I was trained as a violinist. When I get old I'd like to become a professional and play music in the castles in Europe.

∽ Pat, who teaches physical therapy: I'm a good cook and I love people. I'd like to have a bed-and-breakfast.

∽ Ruth, a former attorney: I'd like to put serious time and effort into my sculpture.

∽ Deborah, a writer: I have a book idea I've been thinking about. I've written fiction before, but not in my own voice, in my own name. It feels very important to me; that's what I want to be doing. And I'd like to be making a lot more money.

∽ Rachel, a photographer for a local college: I want to be out on my own, supporting myself with my creative photography.

~ Ellie, an independent health care consultant: I'm thinking about taking a job I just interviewed for. It's less money, but it's an opportunity at a whole new career in sales.

~ Stephanie, an environmental researcher: Sometimes I think about getting clinical training and doing therapy. I'm interested in trauma and how that affects development. I'd like to write a book about becoming disabled in the middle of your life and what that's all about.

~ Elizabeth, a pediatrician: I have this ambition to write plays. There's some desire that's separate from my professional life to achieve something, some recognition or success, as defined by the external world.

Apparently, we're right on schedule. Researchers have found that during midlife, men and women focus on domains we neglected earlier. Women also become more assertive. Our careers are the perfect arena to direct this new vigor. Even if we've held jobs all along, our work becomes a more important source of self-esteem and confidence, especially if we are finally free from child-rearing responsibilities.

In addition, traditional timetables have disappeared. Conventional wisdom is that we go through an orderly series of developmental stages or crises, each with its own physical, emotional, and cognitive tasks. But today, women occupy many roles; we shift back and forth in our timing and commitment to career, marriage, and children. Many of us change jobs or even careers throughout our lives.

At fifty, the biological clock may have run out, but there's a new clock ticking, reminding us that it's our last chance to put our stamp on the world. So, we look for work that challenges us, that allows us to be creative, or gives us the opportunity to do something that matters. Some of us can't realize our aspirations where we are. Rather than stagnate, or remain somewhere comfortable but uninspiring, we decide to risk a change.

Increasingly, we're starting new careers in our forties and fifties. Representative Nancy Pelosi, House minority leader, did not even run for political office until she was forty-seven and the last of her five children had left home. How's that for a model? In addition, during research with women who achieved eminence in their fields between the ages of fifty-five and ninety, Sally Reis, Ph.D., a professor of educational psychology at the University of Connecticut in Storrs, has found that the later years are very productive for the development of women's creativity.

Indeed, we shouldn't let age hold us back, says Heidi Hartmann, Ph.D., president and CEO of the Institute for Women's Policy Research. "If you're fifty-five, and you think it's too late to go to college, think again. The older you are, the longer your life expectancy, so start thinking in terms of living to age ninety. If there's a degree you want to get, go ahead and do it."

Instead of plunging into another career, Rachel has already started on her dream of building a freelance business, using the skills she already has. Her job as a photographer at a local college is fairly routine, but in her spare time she does her own, more expressive photographs. "What I want is to be seen and recognized. At work, I shoot what they want. But with my work, it's about me; it's personal." The more she puts into it, the better she feels. "I've got a studio space now; I'm experimenting with new printing techniques."

Beyond individual achievement, though, there's something else driving us. We want to do work that reflects what we believe in. Marian Ruderman, Ph.D., is a research scientist at the Center for Creative Leadership in Greensboro, North Carolina. In her studies with the organization's Women's Leadership Program for women in middle and senior management, Dr. Ruderman found, "Women have a desire to get their lives better aligned with their values. It's particularly an issue for women in their fifties. They want to do something other than administer widget production, so they move to the nonprofit world or teaching."

Perhaps it's a life-changing illness that propels us to reevaluate. When Marsha developed heart disease, she quit her hospital job. She used her expertise as a nurse to write a book and develop a Web site to help others with the illness. She says, "I'm making a difference in the world, something I've always wanted to do. Connecting with other people. When I get an e-mail from somebody on my Web site, or when I speak with someone and they say that my book has helped them . . . that's what I live for."

We may also change jobs because the personal consequences of the high-power career lifestyle just aren't worth it anymore. When her younger child needed extra tutoring, Amanda's husband offered to take her to the sessions, but it was the final straw for Amanda. "I had thought about leaving for years. Although I was really unhappy, I was afraid to do it. I was the only female vice president. The money, the power, the perks were very seductive. But the workload was awful—my marriage, my work/family scene were so out of balance. I knew if I didn't leave the job now, I'd be so disconnected from my family, I may as well walk out the door. When I finally decided to quit, it wasn't hard. Something had snapped. I just said, 'I'm doing this.' And no regrets." She now works as an independent financial consultant. Though she makes less money, she has the flexibility she wants.

Jill took another approach. After the death of her mate, she decided that life was too short to work sixty to eighty hours a week. "I no longer work weekends or stay in the office till eight at night. I'm never going to be better than I am at what I do, but I've learned over the past few years to really balance it. We only have a certain amount of time, and I'm at an age where I want to have both work and a life."

Some of us find that the workplace is not a benign place for us. Though we're no longer asked how fast we type, sexism and ageism are alive and well, and we may decide we can't take it anymore. The number of age bias complaints filed with the U.S. Equal Employment Opportunity Commission jumped 41 percent between 1999 and 2002. After years in a company, we may be bypassed for a promotion. What's more, many companies have what's called a "pipeline" problem; women aren't hired for positions that lead to the top. The federal Glass Ceiling Commission reports that in most companies, women tend to be in "supporting, staff function areas—personnel/human resources, communications, public relations, affirmative action, and customer relations." In other words, women's work.

When Natalie got divorced, she needed a higher income and benefits, so she signed on as a sales rep in a growing medical company. She had been used to a great deal of autonomy as a nutritionist in a group of alternative medical practitioners and in her work with autistic children. Now, she says, "I have no power. It's frustrating; they want our feedback but they don't implement it. I think it's because it's all men at the top. They have some women who are heads of departments, but the people in power are men, all men." Natalie plans a change. "I envision a part-time clinical consulting role as a nutritionist, maybe continuing to do some speaking. I also want to continue working with autistic kids, which I've been doing a few hours a week. Oh, and I'd like to teach yoga." Although she finds it daunting to think about being her own boss, she knows she can do it.

In some industries, fifty-something women may be kicked upstairs. For example, in book and magazine publishing, management is increasingly hiring staff in their twenties and thirties to save money on high salaries and attract younger readers. A young boss may be disdainful of our experience and think us "uncool." While that hasn't happened to me, I have had to adjust to working for editors who are twenty years my junior.

We may also face more insidious forms of sexism. "Women feel excluded from informal channels of information, which are critical to learning what's valued, what isn't, and what's going on," says Marsha Brumit Kropf, former vice president for research and organization of Catalyst, a nonprofit research group. Out of the loop, we may too easily fall victim to office politics. Diana worked in a large advertising firm where her male mentor had promised her a top job—the corner office with all the trimmings—and then left the company before making it final. "I had been all agog and trusting and wide-eyed. I might have known the new guy would want his own people. But the way he dealt with me was very painful. Instead of just saying, 'I know what was promised, but there is no room for you here, so here's your severance,' he methodically isolated me. I wasn't allowed to go to meetings and people wouldn't talk to me. It was awful."

Even when we're "good girls," the rewards may not materialize. Ellie worked for a large HMO for seventeen years. Because she didn't have a family, she was particularly dedicated. "I believe that single women have this thing about being 'responsible.' We put in the hours because we don't have families. There was a group of us single women who often ended up taking on extra work. Then we realized, what is this about? We were competent and hardworking—I had a job where I had 150 people reporting to me—but we were always 'acting directors.' And this, in a company reputed to be a great place for women."

On the other side of the reward coin, we may be promoted—but to jobs that are not strategically important. Ellie did eventually rise to a national position in her company, although it involved moving to another part of the country. Shortly afterward, though, the company went through a financial crisis and her job was phased out. "The truth was, I'd thought for a while that I should make a change. Too bad I had to be pushed."

Unlike Ellie, many midlife women don't wait to be pushed if we feel unappreciated. Some of us realize that even though we've hoped for years that a job or a career is going to get better, it's not. Others feel we have to hide or suppress part of ourselves, or change our style in ways that are unacceptable in order to remain in hierarchical organizations; we may realize that we're becoming people we don't want to be. So many of us leave, that corporate America is starting to acknowledge it as a problem.

Women are still judged by different standards from men. Jennifer Allyn of Catalyst, quoted in the *AARP Bulletin*, said, "We talk about the fact that women have to be 'overripe' for promotion—they have to demonstrate they can do the next job before they get promoted to it. By comparison, men are promoted much earlier on—when they're hungry, not when [they're] ready." Catalyst notes that 77 percent of top corporate women said they'd made it by exceeding expectations, 61 percent by developing a style with which male managers are comfortable, and 50 percent by seeking out difficult assignments.

It's not that we aren't effective. An article published in 2000 in *Business Week* reported, "By and large, the studies show that women executives, when rated by their peers, underlings, and bosses, score higher than their male counterparts on a wide variety of measures—from producing high-quality work to goal setting to mentoring employees . . . recognizing trends, and generating new ideas and acting on them."

The problem is despite these strengths and the bottom-line results, many women do not feel their collaborative work style is respected. Most of the women Dr. Silverstein studied had had more than two decades of experience. "They all felt as if they'd earned their stripes. But as they moved up in the hierarchy they were 'disappeared.' They were good at team building, collaboration, at leveraging people around them toward the cause. It's a real set of skills, but their skills weren't valued; if anything, they became a liability. They talked about having to take on a persona and play a role they weren't comfortable with."

But we care about relationships, and we know that a collaborative style on the job is productive. "I have a fair amount of power and I'm comfortable with it, but my style is very collegial. I get a good amount of consensus before I proceed," says Trish. At the end of fifteen or twenty years in the workplace, most of the women in Dr. Silverstein's study felt they had earned the right to work in a way they felt was consistent with their best effort. Unappreciated, they left corporate life.

Some started businesses as consultants, and their old clients sought them out. They said, Dr. Silverstein reports, "I liked working with you because you asked good questions, you partnered with me, you told me the truth, you'd tell me when something was a dumb idea. I don't want to hear the party line; I want someone who really works with me." In a short period of time the women were highly successful, and they didn't look back.

However, leaving a powerful, well-paid job is not without its pain. Dr. Silverstein observes, "Women I interviewed felt a sense of personal failure that they hadn't been able to last, and guilt about abandoning young women they were mentoring. They were afraid that men would say, 'See? Look what happens—you bring women in, promote them, and then they leave.'"

And readjustment can take time. At age fifty, Ellie found looking for work in the "new economy" demeaning. "A lot of the jobs were in young, dot-com businesses. I felt passé. Even figuring out what to wear at interviews—I had always worn suits, but these places were more casual. Then there was the age thing. They'd ask, 'You've worked in one place for so long. Are you flexible? Do you think you're creative?'" She didn't work for a year, lost her confidence, got depressed, and gained weight. Through networking, however, Ellie has gotten plenty of work doing health care consulting. And since the collapse of the dot-coms, her résumé is viewed with more respect.

Record numbers of women take the risk and start their own businesses. Today there are more than nine million women-owned businesses, up from 400,000 in 1972. And fifty-something women are often able to make a go of it quickly because of our experience, competence, and, perhaps, an extra shot of ambition, thanks to our age.

Diana didn't choose to leave her job, but she landed on her feet. "I was forced out of the corporate world, which I thought was the only place where I could succeed. But I've started my own small advertising agency, have my own clients, and I create my own projects. I've found a new way to express who I am, and discovered qualities I like about myself but didn't know I had."

When we become our own bosses, we solve some problems but face others. Marlene left her job five years ago to consult with foundations that fund public schools. "When you're self-employed, it's very hard to control the workload. There are periods when I'm working like a lunatic, other times I feel like I'm semiretired and I have to fight to avoid 'the fear.'" Likewise, since I began freelancing twelve years ago, I've developed what I call "freelancers' disease." I don't like turning down work because I'm afraid there won't be enough. Then I find myself drowning in deadlines.

Still, it's worth it. Marlene has four rules: "Do work that matters, work with people I care about, make money, and have fun. I'm getting paid well and I'm happy. I choose what I do. It's a very different dynamic than when you have a boss. There's a lot of pathology in organizations. I'm never going back inside. Never."

retirement? never heard of it

Women who work have better health and higher self-esteem, especially as we get older. That's a good thing, because as we go through our fifties, we may realize that retirement is not around the corner. It's a matter of cold, hard cash. "Have you heard the definition of a woman's needs? From 14 to 40, she needs good looks; from 40 to 60, she needs personality; and I'm here to tell you that after 60, she needs cash," said Mary Kay Ash, as reported in her 2001 obituary.

Many of us are not prepared for retirement. A study reported in *The Wall Street Journal* found that 38 percent of baby boomers report having less than $10,000 in retirement savings. What this means is that what used to be considered the "three-legged stool" of retirement income—savings, pension, and Social Security—will no longer work for us, so we will be staying on the job longer. And we may all be delaying retirement indefinitely, thanks to the stock market "adjustment."

Women are at a distinct disadvantage when it comes to retirement. According to an article in the *New York Times*, income for men over age 65 averages nearly double that for women. Forty-four percent of older female employees cannot expect any pension at all. In addition, if we've worked part-time or interrupted our careers to have kids, our payments from Social Security (assuming it still exists when we retire) will be lower. At least if you're in a conventional marriage, you can get pension benefits from your partner. Lesbian women are not permitted to share retirement income and cannot pass on Social Security benefits to a partner when they die.

By the time many of us enter our fifties, the belief we grew up with—that someone will take care of us—is a shattered illusion. There's nothing like divorce or widowhood to refocus our commitment to work. I can vouch for that, and I'm not alone. In March 2000, 21 percent of women ages forty-five through fifty-four were divorced or widowed; among women fifty-five through sixty-four, the number was 27 percent. So it seems we will be taking care of ourselves.

So, we keep working. The proportion of women in their early sixties still in the workforce is now more than 40 percent, and the rate for women in their late sixties is also rising. Many of us try to play catch-up. To get benefits, Bonnie switched from freelancing to full-time work after her divorce. Still, she despairs of ever being able to retire. "I'm not going to be able to afford to do it." Similarly, Lynette says, "I've changed my adult career three times, so I don't have enough years of service to retire. I keep buying lottery tickets." And because women live longer than men, our money has to last longer. Many women in their fifties who had their children late feel an additional economic squeeze. Laura, who, at 51, adopted a toddler, says, "I know people, my age or a little older, who talk about retirement. But we have to figure out how we're going to pay for preschool, never mind college or retirement."

Even if retirement seems a long way off, we do have our dreams. "I even know my address," muses Marsha. "I want a small apartment in a hotel overlooking Central Park South because it's easy to get to the theater and to Lincoln Center. I plan to do yoga every day. I'll go to Bergdorf's for lunch. I'll have my hair and nails done twice a week." On the other hand, Sue's fantasy involves volunteerism. "If we somehow ended up with lots of money, I'd go to a Third World country and deliver babies, maybe for two months at a time. Besides that, I'd make my own schedule, do quilts, and garden a lot." Sounds good to me.

In forging a new path, we've faced sexism as well as the difficulties of balancing career and family. We are the first generation of women to have serious careers, and our work has given us enormous satisfaction and self-esteem. We reach our fifties with a firm idea of our strengths and abilities, as well as a confident sense of who we are and where we want to go. As Trish says, "I've made it, I can relax now, and I'm still young and fit enough to enjoy it."

Taking Stock and Moving Forward

- As a child, did you expect to work? What did you imagine you'd do?

- Have you always worked in the same career? Did you choose your work, or did you find it through serendipity?

- In addition to income, why do you work now? Is your work a significant source of self-fulfillment for you?

- In your work, what is satisfying, what gives you the most gratification, and what is most difficult?

∽ Have you reached the level you'd like to in your field? If not, what can you do about it?

∽ Are you a workaholic? Do you find that you are living to work rather than working to live? How can you change this?

∽ To what do you attribute your career success? What makes you feel the most competent? List your achievements.

∽ Can you think of ways to do your job that make you more efficient and effective?

facing ourselves

menopause, self-image, and physical health

> *"I told my doctor that after fifty, instead of giving women indi-vidual prescriptions, she should just hand them a bag of pills for high blood pressure, high cholesterol, diabetes, and so on. It'd be like, 'Welcome to the AARP and here's your medicine.'"*
>
> ——Marsha, age 56

PHYSICAL CONCERNS LOOM LARGE during our fifties. Not only do we deal with menopause, but we also face our changing bodies. Perhaps our knees finally give out, making it impossible to continue running, or we develop a chronic illness. Our bodies age in other ways, too, forcing us to adjust to changes in our looks. We begin to pay more at-tention to maintaining our physical appearance and well-being, with a new focus on health, diet, and exercise.

menopause: the false specter

As we move toward fifty, many of us dread the approach of menopause. Take Bonnie, for example, who is just beginning to have some symptoms. "I dread it. I'm worried about shriveling and becoming even shorter than I am, I'm worried about my bones being fragile and breaking, having temper outbursts or permanent PMS. What if I go through a personality change, or a big depression?"

No wonder we have some trepidation. For decades, many researchers and doctors portrayed menopause as a major psychological event. Grounded in Freudian logic, the theory is that a woman's life loses its purpose once she can no longer bear children. Psychoanalyst Helene Deutsch expressed this distorted view in 1945, when she said that with the end of her fertility, a woman "reached her natural end—her partial death."

Other authors have taken this thinking and run with it. Not only do we lose our purpose, they say, we aren't even women any more. In 1969, in *Everything You Always Wanted to Know about Sex But Were Afraid to Ask*, David Reuben, M.D., called menopause "a defect in the evolution of human beings." And in the now-infamous *Feminine Forever*, in which Robert A. Wilson, M.D., promoted heavy doses of estrogen, it wasn't enough for him to describe menopause as "a serious, painful and often crippling disease." No, he went on to say that "castration" and becoming "the equivalent of a eunuch" were what happened to a woman when her estrogen levels dropped. I say, hold the hormones; just give us old crones the cyanide-laced Kool-Aid now, and let's get it over with.

Joking aside, study after study shows that the psychological trauma of coming to terms with our barren wombs simply doesn't occur. As early as 1963, social psychologist Bernice Neugarten, Ph.D., and her colleagues found that "loss of reproductive capacity is not an important concern of middle-aged women at either a conscious or unconscious level." In fact, the middle-aged women in their study looked forward to their postmenopausal years as a time when they'd be healthier and happier.

More recently, in a five-year study of more than 2,500 Massachusetts women, ages forty-five to fifty-five, researchers found that as they experienced menopause, only a small percentage of women reported feeling regret. "Menopause is a blessing in disguise, and that's the best-kept secret," says Erica. "To stop worrying about getting pregnant, to stop worrying about birth control—it's the greatest thing."

I'm not about to pretend that the menopausal transition is easy. The symptoms can be terrible, and they may last for years. If we're uneasy, though, it's not because we're afraid of the symptoms (or of becoming a eunuch). Nor is it because we're disturbed that we can no longer have children (or periods); indeed, for most of us that's a relief. The real bogeyman for fifty-something women is that menopause symbolizes our entry into the last half of our lives. It's another of those clear-cut physical changes that mark a major transition. Beginning to menstruate signals the end of childhood, pregnancy the beginning of parenthood, and now, menopause reminds us that we are not going to escape aging or death. No matter how much we try to control our bodies and our lives, we don't run the show.

Of course, menopause isn't synonymous with old age. Technically the permanent cessation of menstruation, menopause can occur any-time between our thirties to our sixties; it usually occurs between the ages of forty and fifty-eight. In the Western world, the average age is fifty-one. The notorious hot flashes and other symptoms are actually part of perimenopause, or the time leading up to menopause, which may go on for years before our periods actually stop.

We may no longer be young during our fifties, but we are certainly not yet old. On average, if we reach fifty, we can expect to live another three decades, to nearly eighty-two years of age. But, perhaps for the first time, the writing is on the wall.

the reality of menopause

We all have to grapple with menopause. We may have had children at twenty-eight, at forty, or not at all; we may have worked or stayed at home; we may be straight or gay—no matter. We all go through it. Still, our first reaction may be denial. "It took me by surprise because I had just stopped breast-feeding a baby the year before," recalls Sue, a nurse-midwife. "There I was, forty-two, no period. I did a million pregnancy tests, and it never even occurred to me that it could be menopause. Finally I ran some lab tests for hormone levels and even after I saw the results, I still thought, 'This can't be it.'"

Lynette was taken aback by hot flashes. "I thought, 'Oh please. I'm from the tropics, and I probably won't even notice.' But when I was forty-seven, I began waking up with my clothes soaking wet. My body felt like it was burning up from inside." And the duration of the symptoms has been hard for Noreen, who starting going through perimenopause when she was forty-five. "It's much worse and lasted much longer than I ever thought it would. During the ten years I was on estrogen, I felt fabulous. But I didn't want to continue, and I was really surprised that I still had symptoms when I stopped taking it."

But it's not so bad for everyone. For Lola, her symptoms have matched her expectations. "I didn't expect to have a lot of difficulty and I didn't. I've had some hot flashes for about four years, but they're not intense. They're mostly at night, or when I'm at the supermarket," she says, giggling. "There must be something about the air there."

Other women, like Joanne, have been pleasantly surprised. "It's been much easier than I thought it would be."

To put it plainly, though, a lot of women just feel lousy during perimenopause. "It's like childbirth," explains Cathy Miller, a certified nurse-midwife in private practice. "Very few people breeze through it. A large percentage of women have hot flashes, don't sleep well, feel moody, and don't have as much energy. The symptoms ease eventually, but it's varied and individual."

Because estrogen plays many roles in the body, dropping levels can lead to an array of symptoms. Although it's rare for a woman to experience all of them, many of us have at least a few: hot flashes, irregular or heavy bleeding, headaches, insomnia, heart palpitations, dizziness, incontinence, mental fogginess, night sweats, cold hands and feet, facial hair, hair loss, and acne. Of her incontinence, Ruth says, "That's the worst. If you truly want to feel old, if you want to feel just plain miserable, that will do it." She now controls her symptoms with medication and Kegel exercises (contracting the muscles used to stop urination).

Also alarming are symptoms that affect our sex lives, such as painful sex caused by vaginal tissue thinning, drying, or discomfort, and reduced (or nonexistent) sex drive. To combat this problem, many women use vaginal lubricants, vitamin E suppositories, or a vaginal cream with estrogen, which can rejuvenate the tissues in a remarkably short time.

The intellectual and cognitive changes that accompany menopause are more subtle but just as upsetting. Although everyone occasionally has "senior moments" when we can't remember a name, some of us suffer more far-reaching memory loss. Elizabeth frequently experienced times when she couldn't find the right word, or used a word incorrectly, and feared the onset of Alzheimer's. After a battery of tests, she was told it was "just hormones."

According to Ruth Steinberg, M.D., an obstetrician-gynecologist in private practice and assistant clinical professor at the Columbia University College of Physicians and Surgeons, this is not only a female problem. "There is short-term memory loss in menopause, but it's also true in men. It may be that women are more aware of it, or that they are more willing to talk about it. They're more likely to say, 'I'm really starting to lose it.' I think men don't dare say that."

In addition, we may have times when we simply feel fuzzy, like Marlene. "For a while, I had the mental fog thing. Sometimes, I'd be in a meeting and have what I call a 'mentalpause moment.' I tried to use humor to mask it. I'd say, 'Excuse me, but could you back the tape up?'"

The "fuzziness" may be the result of insomnia, another common symptom, but Dr. Steinberg adds that there are other possible causes for our occasional lack of focus. "Fuzzy? I'm not sure how much is just being overwhelmed. Women are jugglers from the get-go—the house, the job, the kids. They always have multiple lists in their heads. If you add to that the many other midlife concerns, such as adolescent children and aging parents, I think the systems get overloaded."

Christiane Northrup, M.D., in *The Wisdom of Menopause*, writes that stress can aggravate hormonal imbalance. Then, menopausal symptoms, like hot flashes and insomnia, exacerbate our fatigue, tension, and irritability. Many women talk about becoming highly emotional, as though they had an extreme version of PMS. "The one thing I remember is the mood swings," says Lynette. I'd get this feeling that I was sad and I didn't know why." Elizabeth talks about being more "volatile," and I certainly have had times when I wanted to jump out of my skin.

Our symptoms are so pervasive that we can easily recognize them in fiction. Novelist Carol Shields described her perimenopausal heroine's feelings in *Happenstance*: "What did this mean, this new impatience, this seething reaction to petty irritations? It could get worse, she saw. You could become crippled by this kind of rage. It was all so wasteful in the long run. And what, she wondered, was the name of this new anger, this seismic sensitivity . . ."

midlife meltdown: hormonal or situational?

Volatility and irritability are not depression; yet, it's widely believed that women suffer more from depression during perimenopause and menopause. In fact, since the 1950s, depression has been included on the checklists of menopausal symptoms used by clinical researchers.

Many believe it's normal for women to be depressed during menopause due to estrogen deficiency. But the evidence just isn't there. In fact, Bonnie Strickland, Ph.D., professor of psychology at the University of Massachusetts in Amherst, feels that the link between depression and menopause is a "myth."

Certainly, depression is disproportionately a female disease: Women are, on average, twice as likely to be depressed as men. Yet, women's rates of depression remain about the same throughout this time of life. Women who are at higher risk for depressive symptoms during menopause are those who go through surgical menopause (hysterectomy); those who are separated, divorced, or widowed; and women with a history of depression.

Among this latter group are women who are "hormonally sensitive," according to Dr. C. Neill Epperson, M.D., a psychiatrist who also does neuroendocrine research at Yale Medical School. She explains, "There are plenty of women who can be estrogen depleted who don't get depressed. But in some women, estrogen depletion or fluctuations in estrogen levels can unmask a vulnerability to depression. This includes women who have had mood symptoms at other times—for example, those who had severe PMS, postpartum depression, or sensitivity to oral contraceptives." And, she says it's the "wackiness" of the changes in hormone levels during perimenopause that are the problem, rather than low levels of estrogen after menopause.

Otherwise, though, if a woman is both depressed and perimenopausal, it's very likely due to other things going on in her life. To wit: We're worried about our health, or we're actually sick. We're worried about our looks. We're coping with our parents. Our children are driving us nuts. Our husbands have left us for bimbos. We hate our jobs. We're not sleeping at night. We can't think straight. We've had a period that lasted three weeks. Need I go on?

the hrt question

What do we use to fight menopausal symptoms? Anything and everything. One night at dinner, a group of us began talking about hot flashes and night sweats, the most common symptoms women experience. Here's what transpired:

GLORIA: My favorite is when I'm talking to someone, usually a man, and the sweat starts pouring down my face.

CORINNE: I keep a fan in my purse and I whip it out in meetings.

JUDITH: Do people understand what you're doing?

CORINNE: I don't care.

JUDITH: That's a great part about being in midlife. You really *don't* care.

CORINNE: I have lots of different fans; here, I'll show you. [She whips a beautiful fan from her purse.]

SUZANNE: During the day, I dress for it; I'm in silk or a shell and a jacket that I can take off and put on. At nighttime I'm lying there, thinking how much I love my comforter, and then I have to whip it off. It's breathe, breathe, breathe, the heat, the heat, the heat, and then it's put the comforter back on.

CORINNE: Has anyone used herbs?

[Yes, the women answer: black cohosh, evening primrose, vitamins . . .]

GLORIA: Last month I went to my gynecologist and told him I'd done everything I could possibly do, and I was ready for a prescription for hormones. Ten days later I get this period from hell. Guess what? I have another appointment tomorrow.

PAT: I cut my hair off, and now I'm letting it grow again. I was waking up drenched.

MARLENE: I had night sweats in my early forties and then I had acupuncture and used Chinese herbs, and they went away.

Conversations like this one are occurring all across America. Most of the women I interviewed have no memories of what their mothers went through. Nor do I. Such things were private then. The very word "menopause" was taboo. But not now. As we go through menopause, we're embracing it the way our generation does everything else. "I learn not just from my friends but from everyone," says Joanne. "The woman at the bus stop, the woman in the cashier's line at the supermarket. You see a woman of a certain age, you look at each other, and all of a sudden you're talking about it."

Sometimes, it seems there's no getting away from it. Newspapers and magazines feature an endless parade of articles and ads for osteoporosis medications, as well as soy products and other natural treatments; when we turn on the TV, we're confronted by model Lauren Hutton discussing her hormone regimen. Been to the health food store lately? There's a host of products, from soy to clover, tailored just for us. Menopause is big business.

Particularly since the summer of 2002, when the news broke that one arm of the hormone replacement therapy (HRT) study—the Women's Health Initiative (WHI)—had been halted because of heightened risk of breast cancer with HRT, we have been thrown into confusion. Despite the results of the study, many gynecologists continue to prescribe HRT for women suffering from severe hot flashes and other perimenopausal symptoms.

But our generation has a history of questioning conventional medicine and taking control of our health care. Remember the women's health movement, *Our Bodies, Ourselves*, and looking at our own cervixes in the 1970s? It's a new chapter in the same story. Most of us will not sit back and allow doctors to make this decision for us.

Because of our concerns about HRT, many of us try other alternatives first. If we're lucky enough, we figure out what works and do it. For example, Stephanie "can't drink alcohol any more—it wakes me up at night—and since I stopped, I sleep much better." And Marlene says, "You know, insomnia is not the worst thing in the world. You get up, read a book, and then go back to bed."

If toughing it out doesn't work, many of us try complementary treatments, such as botanical medicines, acupuncture, or dietary supplements. According to a 1998 survey by the American College of Obstetricians and Gynecologists, menopausal American women visited alternative practitioners more often than conventional doctors. At the suggestion of her midwife, Annie, who has no symptoms yet, is pushing soy. "I religiously eat a tofu salad every day," she says.

The herb black cohosh is popular and is currently under study by the National Institutes of Health. (It's also the leading herbal remedy for menopausal symptoms in Germany.) There are a host of other herbal remedies touted for the relief of physical and emotional symptoms, even though evidence for the effectiveness and safety of most of these supplements is largely anecdotal: red clover, chaste berry (Vitex), and dong quai for "female" symptoms; St. John's wort for mild depression; ginkgo for mental fuzziness; and dietary supplements, such as DHEA, vitamin E, L–arginine, and flaxseed, for decreased libido and a variety of other symptoms.

Some of us do, in fact, feel fine with herbal and dietary supplements. "I use valerian to help me sleep, and it's worked well," reports Noreen. Adds Jill, "I've used black cohosh and Vitex for hot flashes and insomnia, vitamin E for my skin, and ginkgo to clear up the fuzziness. I also make sure I eat a healthy diet and get plenty of exercise. I've been thrilled at how good I feel."

Sometimes, though, we have to bring in the big guns. Natalie, a nutritionist, is very committed to alternative medicine, yet she ended up on hormone replacement therapy. "My hormones stopped responding to the natural stuff. The hot flashes stopped for a few months, but then they got progressively worse, till they were happening every hour. I wasn't sleeping longer than an hour at night. I went on HRT, and it made all the difference." Natalie chose to use an individualized regimen of HRT based on *bioidentical* hormones, whose molecular structure is a precise match for the hormones normally produced by the human body. Bioidentical hormones are available in several forms, including pills and skin patches. They are different from Prempro, a combination of Premarin and Provera (the two synthetic hormones used in the WHI study), but it is not known whether they cause the same negative side effects. They are also the hormones recommended by Dr. Northrup in her book and by many other practitioners.

Like Natalie, most American women turn to HRT for relief of severe physical symptoms. In addition, many of us find that hormone replacement helps even out the mood swings. During the first year after my husband left, I was anxious, depressed, and couldn't sleep. When a friend suggested that some of the misery might be related to perimenopause, I checked in with my doctor. For at least the short term, I've chosen to use bioidentical hormones; it hasn't been a panacea, but it's made a huge difference.

There is some evidence that estrogen can improve mood. According to Dr. Epperson, at Yale, two solid studies show that taking estrogen can relieve depression better than placebo—but only during perimenopause. She says, "I give estrogen as an antidepressant to perimenopausal women who aren't severely depressed, especially if they are having significant menopausal symptoms, such as hot flashes and vaginal dryness. For women who are concerned about the risks associated with using estrogen, the SSRIs [selective serotonin reuptake inhibitors, such as Prozac and Paxil] have been shown to reduce hot flash frequency and severity. These antidepressants are also helpful for mood symptoms that may accompany the menopause transition."

Given that the experts don't even know, how do we decide what to do? Whom can we trust? Our decisions about using HRT are as individual as we are. My friend Teresa, a physician assistant, is, despite the WHI study, adamant that HRT is the right choice for her and most other women. Lola, who made the opposite decision, says, "If Nature had meant for me to continue to have a high level of estrogen, she would have arranged it." And Joanne, who is experiencing more frequent, intense migraines, cannot decide. "HRT may relieve my headaches. The only way to find out is to try. But I'm afraid because it may make them even worse." Noreen decided to stop hormone therapy, with negative results. "The symptoms were awful, worse than before. Night sweats woke me up, I couldn't sleep, I was depressed. Most amazing of all, I lost the ability to have an orgasm. I was floored." Since then, she returned to her gynecologist and compromised on a lower dose. She still has some symptoms, but they are more tolerable. "It's a quality-of-life issue," she says. "I'm taking the risk because I couldn't stand the way I was feeling."

Dr. Steinberg, an ob-gyn, has had many patients go cold turkey with miserable results. "The new information from the WHI is important, but the way it came out was disastrous. It was a disservice to the medical community and the greater community. Most patients don't understand the statistical terms 'relative risk' and 'individual risk.' Those issues are much better dealt with on a one-to-one basis."

menopause has benefits?

Despite the old wives' tales—that's not us!—and myths surrounding menopause, the symptoms, and the quandaries about HRT, research shows that the anticipation is worse than the reality, and that our attitudes toward menopause improve as we actually go through it.

In addition, it may just be that menopause helps us embrace the aging process. At the party I threw for myself one year after my separation, a friend triggered an intense discussion when she said, "Your husband left you because he was afraid of getting old." Her explanation? Hitting fifty comes as a shock to men because they get no warning that they are aging. And when faced with that harsh reality, some men just want to escape; hence, the flying lessons, the younger women, the obsession with Viagra, and so forth.

Women are different. Our bodies' ever-fluctuating hormones keep us in touch with the rhythms of the life cycle. Just as menarche marks our entry into adolescence and adulthood and the ability to create life, the changes of perimenopause are a gradual but no-nonsense reminder that we are no longer able to bear children and that we are aging. Adapting to these shifts keeps us flexible and more able to face change.

What's more, we're probably also aware of our mortality much earlier than men, if only subconsciously. At my party, those of us who were mothers agreed that there's something about bearing a child that puts us in touch with all of life, including its end. "I'm eternally grateful for having given birth," says Joanne. "It's a real gift. One feels more deeply the cycle of life and death." According to psychologist Margot Tallmer, Ph.D., in "The Mid-Life Crisis in Women," when women have children, they experience "the great transformation of narcissism that renders the child's life more precious than their own" and an acceptance of the finite life cycle.

In addition, our changing hormone levels, particularly a sharp increase in testosterone relative to estrogen, contribute to new feelings of vigor and self-assertiveness. We also experience a rise in the hormone GnRH, which in turn precipitates increases in LH and FSH, hormones whose major function had been to stimulate our ovaries to release eggs; LH and FSH levels remain high long after our ovaries have shut down. According to Dr. Northrup, there's evidence that these perimenopausal hormonal changes actually "rewire" the brain, causing changes in the temporal lobe, the area in the brain associated with enhanced intuition. Changes also occur in the hypothalamus, where GnRH is produced. This part of the brain is connected to our experience of anger and other emotions. Hormones also affect the amygdala and hippocampus, which are involved with anger, hunger, sexual desire, and memory. As Dr. Northrup puts it in her book, our brains "catch fire" at menopause. The result? We become more intuitive, more likely to reexamine our lives, and possessed of a new clarity of vision. Of the woman entering menopause, Dr. Northrup writes, " . . . She becomes freer to choose where she will direct her creative energies, freer to 'color outside the lines.' Many of the issues that had become blurry to her when the hormones of puberty kicked in may suddenly resurface with vivid clarity as those hormones recede."

These biochemical changes encourage us to reconnect with ourselves, delve into the past, grieve over unresolved issues, and then get on with our lives. Dr. Northrup likens this time to the PMS-induced urge to clean that many of us used to experience, but on a larger and more internalized scale. As we clean up our lives, we may change relationships, jobs, and marriages in the process. Although there's a lot to get through, this can be an invigorating time. In a 1997 survey by the North American Menopause Society, more than half of American women aged forty-five to sixty viewed menopause as the beginning of a new and fulfilling stage of life. Right on!

our bodies, our selves

As we approach our fifties, regardless of how we feel, each of us has to face what Elvis Costello called "a deep dark truthful mirror." Even though we know it's coming, aging still takes us by surprise. In Michael Cunningham's novel, *The Hours*, we hear Louis's thoughts as he looks at his fifty-something friend Clarissa: "She looks older, Louis thinks in astonishment. It's finally happening. What a remarkable thing, these genetic grip wires, the way a body can sail along essentially unaltered, decade after decade, and then in a few years capitulate to age."

Our bodies begin to look and feel like strangers. "My body is not the same," says Ruth. "It's loosened up. No matter what I do, my muscles don't get tight the way they used to. My stomach hangs a little, just sort of sagging. Does it bother me? Not terribly, but probably more than a lot of people because I was an athlete for so long and my physical being is a large part of who I am."

In addition to drooping, we begin to see wrinkles, age spots, graying and/or thinning hair. Our eyes change. Many of us need glasses for the first time. "I'm very myopic," says Elizabeth, "worse than anyone I know. I've always been able to reach twenty-twenty with corrective lenses, but I'm no longer able to. I have half a dozen different glasses for different occasions, and I never see perfectly."

We've entered the twilight zone, where we feel younger on the inside than we look on the outside. When I asked her how old she felt, fifty-six-year-old Diana answered, "Sometimes I think of the physical me as being seventy, but the real me is about twenty-six." Adds Lynette, "I notice that my hands look wrinkled, but it's not a problem because I don't feel old. I do my treadmill and I bike and I love to go to basketball games. I plan to stay like this as long as I can." Most of us do feel younger than we are. In their book-length study of more than 1,300 people, *Of Human Bonding*, sociologists Alice S. Rossi, Ph.D., and Peter H. Rossi, Ph.D., reported that among men and women with an average age of fifty-five, the women reported feeling twelve years younger than they were. (Interestingly, the men, on average, felt four years older.)

Thanks to exercise and healthy diets, many of us, like Amanda, look young, too. "When I tell people I'm fifty, a lot of them say, 'What? I was sure you were thirty-five or forty.'"

When we do start to look older, we hope the changes will go away, like a bad hair day. "When I face the mirror, I keep thinking that one day I'll look and my own youthful body will be back," muses Joanne. "Or that I'm passing through another stage, much like puberty, and that I'm going to move into another, better stage, which won't be continuing decline. But I know it's a fantasy." Still, as we grow more comfortable with ourselves, we come into our fifty-something looks. Stephanie says, "I look at my friends as they age and I think that they're beautiful."

keeping up appearances

Many midlife women complain about the "invisibility" they begin to experience sometime in their fifties. Around her fiftieth birthday, Alice noticed a change in the courtroom. "I remember the moment when I no longer had anybody's attention. My hair had gotten grayer, and there had been other changes, too. There were a bunch of us women who had gone into practice at the same time. All of a sudden, the judges couldn't tell us apart. We all looked the same to them. It was very disturbing." Dr. Steinberg confirms Alice's sentiments: "We're not a society that reveres our elders, so particularly for women it becomes an issue of marginalization and diminishment."

Marsha refuses to go quietly into oblivion. "I eat regularly with a group of four women, all food professionals, all middle-aged. We were trying a new restaurant and the chef visited every table but ours. And then the owner went to every table but ours." She asked to see the chef and made a point of introducing herself and her friends and complimenting the food. "Women at a certain age shouldn't just grumble about this; we should do something to make it different," she says.

On the other hand, some women like becoming less visible. Of her interview with actress Frances McDormand, Joan Acocella wrote in *The New Yorker*, "When young men stop looking at you, she tells me, this is a loss, but also a gain: You stop looking at yourself through their eyes. As she approached her forties, she decided, 'Oh, fuck it, already. I'll just be. I just am.'"

Ironically, women who have never felt especially attractive may have an advantage now. "There are women who've been valued all their lives for their looks," says Marlene, "and some who have not. I was overweight, so I relied more on my intelligence. I may have felt envy as a young person toward women who were thin and pretty. But it's an advantage as a middle-aged woman not to have relied on my looks. Aging doesn't really hurt me in the same kind of way. I don't keep looking in the mirror, seeing things fade away. In this culture, to be able to look at yourself and feel okay, you have to feel good from the inside out."

And let's face it: Our bodies do change. Wrinkles, added pounds, drier skin, and graying hair affect how we feel about ourselves, especially given our society's strong cultural bias toward youth. It's hard, even for highly intelligent, terrific women, not to buy into it. "My arms have a mottled quality now," says Stephanie, "and I don't want to wear short-sleeved or sleeveless shirts because I don't like the way they look. There is something about youth that is beautiful. A twenty-year-old can not be very pretty and still be beautiful. Even their skin is pretty, you know?"

What rankles about aging is our society's double standard. Observes Lola, "You'd have to be drop-dead gorgeous to be noticed, and even then people would say, 'You know she's pushing sixty?' They'd never say that about a man; they'd never say, 'Damn, that Paul Newman looks good, can you believe he's in his seventies?'" The older we get, the worse it is. Older men can be "suave" or "sexy" (think Sean Connery); we're just old and wrinkled (think Wicked Witch of the West).

As Joanne puts it, "In our culture, many people think, 'For a sixty-year-old woman, she's attractive,' but that proviso is always there." That's a shift she's not willing to make. "I think of myself as handsome. I have a strong sense of self, and of who I am, and I don't allow myself to be judged that way."

Of course, many of us, like Amanda, never felt attractive enough. "I was never quite where I wanted to be, I was always ten pounds off or a bad haircut away," she says. Ironically, now, when she feels that time is running out, she realizes how good-looking she was and still is. "I feel like I don't have much longer to be the most attractive woman I could be, and I'm making the most of what I've got. When I look back at pictures of myself, I wonder why wasn't I happy with my looks. It isn't just lost youth, it's a loss of something you could have felt good about all along. And when I'm eighty and looking at pictures of me at fifty-five, I'm sure I'll be just as surprised."

Coming to terms with our looks and finding new, inner sources of self-esteem may be particularly hard for women who have always been able to turn men's heads, whose sense of their own power and worth came from their outward appearance. "It's almost like I want to take my shower in the dark," admits Pat. "Really. Lying in the Jacuzzi, I think, 'This used to be a great body that I liked to show off.' Now I wouldn't dream of it."

Issues of appearance may be more than skin-deep. Combine self-image with some of the physical and emotional changes of menopause, and you may have a real problem. Nurse-midwife Cathy Miller points out, "Look at *Time* magazine, look at TV, look anywhere—older women are not made to feel attractive. As a result, they also don't feel as sexy. If I see fifteen older women in one day, I'd say thirteen come in complaining of decreased libido." What's more, says Dr. Steinberg, "Women are not supposed to be sexually oriented anyway, so God forbid that older women should be thinking about it."

And there's nothing like having pretty daughters to drive home the point that we are no longer in the spotlight. "I've always been attractive and liked being attractive," says Noreen. I've had periods in my life when I walked into a room and everybody looked, and I liked that.

Now, of course, it happens less. If I walk down the street with my daughter, people look at her. I'm not jealous or competitive. But it's hard not to be the one everyone looks at."

mirror, mirror on the wall

Many of us start to spend more time on our appearance. By the time we're sixty, we may color our hair and choose our makeup with the aim of looking younger. "It's all about maintenance after fifty," says Erica. "There is no way I could deal with the world if I didn't feel the kind of confidence that comes from my blond hair, courtesy of L'Oreal, and my makeup and from being slim. And I've gotten more dramatic about the way I look and dress."

Making sure we look the way we want to look takes more attention. Noreen explains, "Clothes don't fit the same. I used to be able to buy off the rack, to put something on and walk out. I knew what size I was, knew what style would look great. Now, I have to try everything on, so I spend much more time on my appearance than I ever did before. But I don't mind. It makes me feel good when I can look in the mirror and think, 'You look great.'"

But those of us who consider ourselves feminists are conflicted about accommodating our culture's view of older women. "I put more energy into my appearance now," says Stephanie, a self-described "aging feminist." "I get my forty-dollar haircut and I highlight my hair. I wear a little bit of makeup, which I didn't for years, and I put moisturizer on my skin. I pay some attention to how I dress. But I hate it. I feel like we don't have a handle on this."

Still, most women want to look as good as they can. And fortunately, in our fifties we usually have more time and money to devote to it, if we so choose. At this point in life we've often arrived at our own style: We know the kind of clothes and makeup that are flattering. We've hit on hairstyles that become us. We care for our skin. We used to feel the need to do this for our jobs, but the focus may be changing. Now we want to look good for ourselves. We want to be able to look in the mirror and be pleased.

Laura feels more attractive at fifty-four than she ever did. "I always hated my very curly hair, but I finally found a hairdresser who taught me how to make it look curly instead of frizzy. Since learning how to deal with my hair, I've changed my whole look. I used to wear loafers and a blazer; now I experiment with clothes, too. I have a much more positive sense of myself."

Women who consider cosmetic surgery usually do so for the first time in their fifties (though most of the women I spoke with wouldn't do it). The field is growing dramatically. According to the American Society for Aesthetic Plastic Surgery, there was a 304 percent increase in cosmetic surgical and nonsurgical procedures performed between 1997 and 2001, with over 8.5 million procedures in 2001. Lipoplasty (liposuction) went up 118 percent, tummy tucks by 109 percent, cosmetic eyelid surgery by 55 percent, and face-lifts by 18 percent. Botox (botulinum toxin injections), used for the treatment of frown lines, forehead furrows, crow's feet, and wrinkles of the lower face, was the number one procedure overall, up by a staggering 2,356 percent to 1,600,300 procedures in 2001. Women accounted for 88 percent of the cosmetic procedures.

After a divorce and a career change, Marsha had cosmetic surgery to remove her stretch marks and the large pores ("craters," she calls them) on her nose. She's "thrilled" and is contemplating other procedures. Two of the women I interviewed had breast reduction surgery (although their procedures were as much for comfort as appearance). Jill, a widow, reports, "The creases from my nose to my mouth were making me look old, and I was beginning to feel unattractive. I decided to have a face-lift, and it's changed my whole outlook on life. It's not just that men are looking at me again—I couldn't care less— it's that *I* like the way I look again."

Fortunately, cultural attitudes toward youth and beauty are changing. A *New York Times* article reported that there is a "growing parade of middle-aged screen lovers" in movies that "try to project an optimistic view of middle age as not a sad inevitability but as yet another of life's passages—and a sexy one at that." Think about Sally Field, Charlotte Rampling, Meryl Streep, Diane Keaton, Sissy Spacek, Bette Midler, Goldie Hawn, and Jessica Lange, fifty-something actresses who remain vibrant and attractive, or the stunning gray-haired models that have begun to appear in Eileen Fisher ads and various clothing catalogs.

Many women continue to feel good-looking despite the physical changes associated with menopause. In a 1997 survey by the North American Menopause Society, six in ten women did not associate feeling less attractive with menopause. In fact, some of us find middle age liberating. We may take a page from novelist Dorothy Sayers. In reply to men who complained that trousers on women were unbecoming, she said, "If the trousers do not attract you, so much the worse; for the moment I do not want to attract you. I want to enjoy myself as a human being."

It's not only about being attractive to men; it's about realizing that the hallmarks of old age can be beautiful. Diana, who has a full head of striking white hair, says, "When I was in my early forties, my hair turned white. So I colored it for years. Then I woke up one morning and decided to take a stance. I'm not going to be forced into the beauty parlor every three weeks to dye my hair red. I'm in my fifties, and I have white hair. This is the way I look."

Similarly, Dorothy, a black belt in karate, wears her age proudly. "I go to tournaments, and the only people my age who compete are men. I used to use henna, and I always made sure that I did the henna before the tournament. Now I make sure the gray is showing. I get a lot of respect."

By redefining ourselves, looking our best, and refusing to fall victim to men's standards of youthful good looks, we come up with our own definition of beauty that takes our feelings of self-confidence, assertiveness, and self-knowledge into account. Feeling good about how we look is the key.

our "growing" concerns

One of the most common, and unwelcome, changes—but one that we can do something about—is weight gain. As we approach menopause, our waistlines thicken, and our bellies and thighs may become heavier. As a result of a slowdown in metabolism, we may gain between ten and twenty pounds, even if we're not eating more than before. "I don't like being twenty pounds overweight, and I'm working so hard to lose it," says Sue. "I don't remember ever working this hard before. I love to eat and until five or six years ago, I was always able to eat whatever I wanted."

Those of us who are thin don't escape. In the year before my ex-husband left, I had slowly moved up to 129 pounds, more than I had ever weighed before. Divorce turned out to be an efficient method of weight loss, although I certainly don't recommend it.

Weight gain is especially problematic for women who were already heavy. "Women who were overweight can now become very heavy, which is dangerous to their health," says nurse-midwife Miller. "It behooves [health care] providers to try to push exercise and diet for women in their forties, because their weight jumps in their fifties."

Extra pounds may put us at increased risk for chronic illnesses, such as heart disease, breast cancer, uterine cancer, diabetes, kidney stones, hypertension, arthritis, polycystic ovary disease, urinary incontinence, gallstones, stroke, and sleep apnea. And once we are through menopause, we are also at higher risk for heart disease and osteoporosis. Of course, the good news is that weight gain is something that is under our control. Through consultation with a nutritionist we can learn to eat in ways that will allow us to shed unwanted pounds and also keep the weight off.

Unlike Garrison Keillor, who once said, "I believe in looking reality straight in the eye and denying it," many of us are paying more attention to maintaining our physical well-being. For example, a recent survey of baby boomers done by *My Generation* magazine found that one in four midlife women is on a weight-loss diet now, and another 23 percent say they will be in the future.

Myra's waistline slowly expanded when she started a new, more sedentary job doing research and put on fifteen unwelcome pounds. "I go out walking early every morning, and I'm doing Weight Watchers online," she says. "I'm losing a pound a week with no trouble."

Of course, dieting isn't easy for everyone. "In my family, everyone was always dieting," recalls Rachel. "It was a constant, horrible mind-set—don't eat too much, you're too fat . . ." Like many women of all ages, Rachel has an ambivalent relationship to food. She says her worst times are when she's feeling fat; yet, when asked what she does to cope, she laughed, "I eat. I eat and I cry."

Sometimes, considering a diet is as close as we get. "Of course, I think I should diet," says Elizabeth. "My cholesterol is higher than it should be, but my good cholesterol is great, so I'm ambivalent. When I eat ice cream now, I think, 'Elizabeth, you shouldn't be eating this.' Does it stop me? No."

Usually, however, the time comes when health considerations make us serious about shedding the pounds. Marsha had dieted off and on her whole life. Several years ago, though, she was told she had high cholesterol. That, and watching her mother cope with the consequences of severe diabetes, compelled her to get into shape. "I simply decided that my health and well-being were the top priority in life. I lost fifty-seven pounds, and there's not a day when I don't exercise."

And when all else fails, humor gets us through. "I pay incredible attention to my diet," says Joanne, "but I often lose the battle. I don't want to go up another underpants size, and who can afford to buy more clothes? I always wondered how my mother could wear expando elastic waistlines. But now I thank God for Lycra."

fitting in fitness

When it comes to exercise, the biggest problem we face is finding the time. Joanne gets up early to go to the gym every morning before her commute to work. "If I want to have a life with my partner and my friends, or to do something other than work, either I only get six hours of sleep or I don't exercise. I know it's important, so I am doing it, but it takes so much time, and it seems very hard."

Still, we try to fit exercise in because there are such enormous payoffs. It makes us feel good and gives us more energy. An hour a day of moderate-intensity activity helps us shed pounds and keep them off, and even thirty minutes on most days reduces the risk of heart disease, strokes, diabetes, and some cancers. When we're fit, we recover more quickly from an illness or surgery. After a hysterectomy, Dorothy rebounded rapidly because she was in great shape from her years of karate. "All the breathing that I'd learned, the ability to sustain stress and pain through mental control, came into play. The belief that my energy would come back, the concentration, the determination—I put all of that into recovering. People told me I wouldn't walk for five days, and I was up after three."

In addition, exercise may be an antidote for lowered libido. Susan Lark, M.D., author of numerous books on women's health, writes in her "Women's Health Update," "I have found aerobic exercise and yoga stretches can enhance sexual desire and performance . . . Simply taking a 20- to 30-minute walk every day, at a moderate pace, can improve your sex drive."

Exercise is also such a great antidepressant, someone once referred to it as "Nature's Prozac." There's plenty of research on the subject, and I know about it from my own experience. In the year after my husband left, I tried to do some kind of exercise—running, yoga, weight training at the gym—every day. The blues were worse when I didn't.

An excellent way to improve mood, and relieve stress, is yoga. There are now an estimated 18 million people doing yoga in the United States, and most of them are women. While some of us have been doing it for years, many fifty-something women take it up because yoga is kinder to aging knees and hips than other kinds of exercise. In addition, it enriches us spiritually and emotionally. "Yoga really helps because even at eighty, you can still be flexible, and feel young and vital," says Suzanne, a teacher. "That vitality is key. Vitality is the word for me this year." Marion, who teaches yoga, adds, "I'm in better physical shape than I ever used to be."

The bottom line is, exercise helps us feel good about ourselves. Rachel, who walks almost every day and lifts weights a couple of times a week, agrees. "I like that I'm strong. I really feel better and I look better."

serious business

As our fifties dawn, most of us become more concerned about our health. "I was out with a group of women from high school," recalls Marlene, "and everyone was talking about their colonoscopies and their mammograms. I thought, 'Oh, please, why are we having this conversation? Can't we talk about movies, books, *anything* else?'"

Many of us don't fear death as much as aging poorly. Joanne has seen both of her parents die. She is healthy and active, but worries about slowly getting old, incapacitated, and, worst of all, dependent on her children. "Since Daddy died of Alzheimer's, I don't for one minute feel I'm going to escape mental incapacity—it's my worst fear about getting older. No, my worst fear is being impoverished and having to be in a hideous situation that's painful to me and my children. I have no doubt they will have to make decisions around me, but I'd at least like them to not have to take care of me at home." Adds Joanne with an ironic grin, "The last time she moved, my daughter joked, 'Ma, the good thing is we're close to a nursing home.'"

Nevertheless, illness and death are becoming all too real. An acquaintance of mine had a massive heart attack and bypass surgery a couple years ago. Several of the women I interviewed had had a friend or friends die of breast or ovarian cancer. And Gail was herself diagnosed with breast cancer one month after being widowed. "Knock on wood, I'm seven years out," she says today, after having had a lumpectomy and radiation treatments.

We may spend our time worrying about cancer only to be sideswiped by something utterly unexpected. Five years ago, at age fifty-four, Ruth, an amateur sculptor, was diagnosed with Parkinson's disease. "It makes it hard to do a lot of things. It makes me clumsy, I trip." As a former athlete, coping with the disease is especially poignant. "I'm losing more than just my physical ability to do things—I'm also losing my self-image." Grasping her new reality comes very slowly. She adds, "The process of a disease that's degenerative is very final. Even if they figure out how to stop the disease, they won't be able to put back the pieces I've lost. On days when I have no tremor, I forget that I have it and think it must be a misdiagnosis. You don't come to terms with it all of a sudden; it's a gradual realization and acceptance, and I'm certainly not there yet."

Accepting limitations is also difficult for Rachel, who's having trouble with her hearing. "I can't tell you what it was like to finally go and get a hearing aid. It was an enormous event filled with anger, denial, and, I guess, a sense of humiliation."

Likewise, Lynette was depressed for a month after her diagnosis of diabetes. "I'd be okay, as long as I was busy at work. But the minute I walked through my door, I'd collapse on the couch, where I'd spend the whole evening." Then she remembered an old friend and her sister, both of whom have the disease. "I thought, 'They're going on with their lives. What's the matter with me?'"

But Lynette didn't take her disease lying down. She rallied. She's gotten her diet-and-exercise regimen under control and has the information she needs at her fingertips. "I must have two shelves of health books. When something comes up, I do research. I'm on the Internet now," she says. Similarly, Ruth does yoga and Pilates to maintain her strength and flexibility.

Stephanie is a great example of someone who has successfully accommodated a painful disability. Hit by a car about fifteen years ago, her fused neck and lower back cause chronic pain, and she can't do everything she'd like. "There are things I don't do: I don't run, even though I'd love to; I would never ski; I don't horseback ride; I didn't take a long drive the other day to visit friends because I knew my neck would tense up." Yet, her life is so busy; with a full-time job, a college-age daughter, and a full-to-bursting social life, you'd never know she has any problems. Rather than resenting what she misses, she's happy for what she has. "I walk forty-five minutes to an hour a day, I do Pilates two times a week, and I do exercises the other days. Two hours of my day are spent exercising, and I have to do that, but it's okay. I love it because I couldn't do it for years."

Even if we are hale and healthy, many of us still fret about changes. For the first time, our bodies may not easily do everything we expect. Perhaps the first twinges of arthritis are making it harder to get out of bed. Or we've developed back problems. "Every time I get out of a car I'm stiff," says Elizabeth, "and if I drive for more than an hour, getting out of the car is painful. I have to walk slowly." Natalie, a marathon runner, notices other, more subtle changes. "I was used to having an athlete's body, but I'm slowing down; I don't have as much stamina as I used to."

By the time we reach our fifties, chances are we've learned that we can't control our parents, our bosses, our children, or our spouses. Now we learn that our bodies follow their own rhythms, too. Still, much depends on how we look at the face in the mirror.

TAKING STOCK AND MOVING FORWARD

∞ Are you troubled by hot flashes or other perimenopausal symptoms? In addition to your gynecologist, talk to your friends; they may have found useful remedies.

- If your mother is still alive, ask her about her menopause to give you clues about what you can expect.

- Is your libido suffering? Are you exercising? A little pampering can also help. A massage, a facial, a trip to a spa, a new kimono?

- Are you satisfied with the face and figure that greet you in the mirror each morning? If not, take steps to do something about it. Diet? Exercise? More rest? A refreshed wardrobe? A new haircut?

- Experts recommend that we eat five to nine servings of fresh fruit and vegetables a day to stay healthy and prevent chronic diseases. Can you add more fresh produce to your diet?

- Do you have a daily exercise regimen in place? If not, start one now. Aim for thirty minutes a day. Try meeting a friend every morning for a walk or run before work. Or try the "lifestyle" model, incorporating several ten- to fifteen-minute periods of exercise into your daily routine, e.g., climbing stairs instead of taking the elevator, gardening or doing yard work, taking a brief walk at lunchtime.

the buddy system

our friendships

" . . . I appreciate my friends and their absolute and irreplaceable importance in my life. They have become both the curators of my past and the guardians of my future."

—Margot Livesey, "The Valley of Lost Things"

ON THE WORST MORNING of my life, when I came home to a disembodied man's voice on my answering machine, telling me about my husband's affair, I could barely stand up. In a state of shock, the first thing I did was call my best friend.

I have no doubt: I would not have made it through the last three years without my friends. Friends gave me innumerable dinners, shoulders to cry on, advice on how to deal with my daughters and my ex, and they talked me through horrible spells of anxiety and depression. They gave me support and boosted my morale.

They supplied calming perspective. When I moaned to a friend that I felt like screaming, that I was being tested, and that nothing ever got better, she said, "You are indeed being tested. You're incredibly stressed, but you're doing fabulously well on the Karen's Coping Inventory measure of day-to-day functioning, and also on the Baar Test of Basic Skills that predicts long-term outcomes. Go ahead and scream, but know that things will work out." (Need I explain that she's a psychologist?) Most important, though, friends helped me laugh.

profound connections

Psychologist Carol Gilligan, Ph.D., psychiatrist Jean Baker Miller, M.D., and other researchers maintain that our sense of self is organized around our ability to make and maintain relationships. While a man typically depends on one person, usually a woman, to meet his needs for intimacy, we often share our feelings with a network of people.

Unlike family, our friends see us as we are now, rather than frozen in old roles, like images in a family album. By the time we reach our fifties, longtime friends also provide valuable continuity, a memory bank that helps us reflect on and evaluate our lives.

Emotionally and otherwise, friends come through during troubled times. Consider Stephanie. She suffers periodic flare-ups from chronic neck and back problems since a long-ago car accident. Divorced and on her own for many years, she says, "My friends have rallied around me. A few years ago, when my neck went out, they instantly got in gear. They organized somebody to bring me dinner every night and figured out who would take me to my medical appointments."

On occasion, friends bail us out financially. After a long struggle with her business, Gail, a widow, was finally able to buy a condominium, but she couldn't get a mortgage because of her financial history. "God bless her soul, my friend bought it for me and held the mortgage. After two years, I was able to get a mortgage in my own name."

Friends also help us clarify our thinking. I needed a surgical procedure several months ago. While chatting with a friend over coffee, I realized that I was leery because the surgeon had just finished her residency and was so young. "I'd get a second opinion, or I'd ask around about her, if I were you. It may be minor surgery, but it's still your body," she said. Until I talked with her, I hadn't acknowledged how dubious I was feeling.

We turn to friends for feedback, input, and to help us examine every side of a problem or decision. A good friend provides the necessary context when we can't see the forest for the trees. "I have to rebuild my life from scratch, and I don't know how to begin," I remember saying to one of my closest friends. "You're already doing it," she replied. And she was right.

A close relationship with a woman friend is emotionally rich, multi-layered, and complex. "It's someone you love and care about, who loves and cares about you," says Joanne. "There's always something to talk about, whether it's just yapping or something of substance. You want to be a part of her life, and you want her to be a part of yours. You enjoy doing things together, being able to argue about things, to disagree, and then find a way to come back together. You may have periods when you're close and others when you're more distant, but there's always the mutual understanding that this relationship will endure."

As we go through the many transitions of life in our fifties, our friends help us redefine ourselves. Not only do they comfort and confront us, but they also provide a sounding board, a place to play out our fantasies. "They provide that safe, comfortable, nonthreatening space to explore what can be terrifying questions," explains Millie

Grenough, a psychotherapist and performance coach in New Haven, Connecticut. "You can feel as miserable as you want, dream as many 'wild' dreams as you want, and they won't tell you, 'That's stupid, you could never do that.' Being able to spin out what you would like to do is so important. If you don't get the chance to dream about it, it doesn't have a chance to be born."

Close friends are also precious because they can listen uncritically. "My best friend lets me say things that are unspeakable, and she doesn't judge me for it," says Rachel. "When I talked to her about all the terrible things going on with my parents—how sick and miserable they were—I said, 'You know, the good news is, they're going to die; the bad news is, not soon enough.' It was that kind of thing; it was okay to admit to her I wished they would die." When friends love us even after hearing our worst thoughts, it eases our feelings of shame and lets us feel better about ourselves.

Exposing ourselves this way is mutually empowering. In *A Woman's Journey to God*, psychologist Joan Borysenko, Ph.D., describes it in almost spiritual terms: "As we come to trust a friend, we reveal more of ourselves. Our idealized mask falls off as we realize that she loves us, warts and all. We can be ourselves. And in being listened to with an open heart, a deeper sense of self actually emerges. What may have been unconscious comes into the light of awareness. We know ourselves better. We become more authentic and wise . . . Once again, we find ourselves anointed with the nectar of divine belonging."

the lighter side

Of course, friendships aren't all heavy conversation and soul-searching. Nor are all friends best friends. There are many levels of friendship. In *Just Friends*, Lillian B. Rubin, Ph.D., draws a distinction between "friends of the road," or people who pass through your life, and "friends of the heart," those relationships that are long-lived and continuous. I'd also distinguish between "true," "close," or "best" friends, and others. Marlene adds, "There are people you can call or who can call you at three in the morning, and then there are friends you just go and have dinner with."

We may do nothing more than play tennis with one woman, while someone else is our partner in crime when we need a dose of retail therapy. In addition, different friends bring out different qualities: With one, we may feel motherly; with another, like a sister; and with someone else, like a giggling schoolgirl.

Many of us have friends who are part of our everyday lives. There are two women with whom I check in through e-mail or by telephone almost every day, and another I talk to at least once a week for an hour. We catch up on what's going on in our lives and generally chew things over. These relationships are reminiscent of what author Vera Brittain wrote of her friendship with Winifred Holtby in *Testament of Friendship*: "Neither of us had ever known any pleasure quite equal to the joy of coming home at the end of the day after a series of separate varied experiences, and each recounting these incidents to the other over late biscuits and tea."

And I won't deny that women gossip. Reading Jane Smiley's description in "Can Writers Have Friends?" made me feel much less ambivalent about this often-maligned activity: "Gossip is about the understanding and assimilation of daily events. There are five stages of gossip. They are: wait-till-you-hear-this (information), are-you-kidding (amazement), I-can't-stop-thinking-about-it (fascination), you-know-why-she-did-it-don't-you (speculation), and actually-I'm-not-a-bit-surprised (understanding). Every pair or group of gossipers is constructing a piece of fiction by making a logical character out of a mysterious person, or a logical story out of an untoward event. The story that emerges after all the facts are known and fitted in is, in my opinion, often a work of collaborative oral art, which I would define as life reworked by thought."

Moreover, it's not just girls who want to have fun, as the song goes. Fifty-something women do, too. We get down, dirty, and silly with our friends. In my book group, we have meaningful, intellectual conversations about serious books. We also made *Valley of the Dolls* our selection last August. We watched the movie at our meeting that month, giggling and popping M&M "dolls." Regardless of what we read, our sessions often end in sidesplitting free-for-alls about sex, and scintillating topics such as Hollywood's latest scandal or couple-of-the-moment. Who wore what to the Oscars is also of critical significance. In her short story, "What Is Remembered," Alice Munro might have been describing us: "A lightening of spirits when the husbands departed. Dreamy rebellion, subversive get-togethers, laughing fits that were a throwback to high school . . ."

friends and partners, men and women

Friends don't take the place of partners. "There's something about being in bed with someone every night and having your ankles crossed or your butts touching that's very intimate—that, obviously, I don't have with my friends," notes Elizabeth.

But women offer a different kind of support. "Stewart won't talk to me when I'm upset about certain things," continues Elizabeth. "He can't be as thoughtful or he doesn't want to pay attention because he gets anxious, so he'll tell me he doesn't want to discuss it. That's when I call a friend." Rather than trying to get blood from a stone, as the saying goes, we get support from our friends. That way, we can appreciate what our husbands can give us, instead of dwelling on what they can't.

Besides, partners can be too close to be helpful. Noreen says, "I talk to my husband about nearly everything, but there are things we don't talk about because he can't stand seeing me upset, or I've talked about it too much and he doesn't have the patience," says Noreen, who's been married to Frank for thirty-three years. "My female friends don't have that same feeling; they're more accommodating. One person can't give you everything you need."

Marlene agrees. "Being friends with women is like being part of a club. There's a lot of stuff you don't have to explain. I don't meet many men who have in-depth knowledge about women, even when they're in a couple. There's a way that we're still unknown and mysterious to them."

I used to think my husband was my best friend—but friends, especially women friends, offer another way of listening. "Women bounce feelings onto and through their friends," says psychologist Ruthellen Josselson, Ph.D., coauthor of *Best Friends*. "They put emotions out on the table, sift them together, think of other possibilities. It's more than advice, it's sharing. Men are mystified by this process of sifting through."

Indeed, researchers have found that women and men have distinct styles of friendship. Male friendships are based on shared activities, while women's are built on shared feelings. Dr. Josselson explains, "The central difference is doing versus being. Men do friendship differently; for them, it's not a shared emotional construction of life. Still, that doesn't mean it's less meaningful for them." Men do bond, despite their lack of intimacy.

Women, however, are often amazed by what men *don't* discuss. My friend Jessica reported: "My husband's best friend was going through a divorce; his wife had left him, and he was a wreck. Whenever he'd call, I'd ask how he was doing, how his kids were, how he was feeling. But when my husband got on, they'd talk about soccer."

The men I know talk about work, sports, family, or women, but only to a point. Too much self-disclosure is risky. Just how risky was clear when Dr. Rubin interviewed 300 men and women between ages twenty-five and fifty-five for her book *Just Friends*. Of those who were married or living with a partner, she asked who they'd turn to if they came home and their partner announced he or she was leaving. Every woman named at least one friend, but, she writes, "most men sat in an uneasy silence for what seemed like a long while. When they finally found their voice, they spoke hesitantly as they realized there was no friend to whom they would turn at such a moment, none to whom they would reveal their anguish."

But many men do have close friendships with us. Often, we become friends with male colleagues, the husband or mate of a friend, or with an old lover. If he's a man in a couple with whom we socialize, however, it can be sticky. "I'm close friends with a man who used to be my law partner," says Annie, "but his wife is threatened by our friendship. He's an attractive, charismatic guy, but he's also very monogamous and loyal. I used to go up to their beach house, but that stopped when I realized she couldn't handle it. But he and I are still close; we talk or e-mail every day."

Many women I spoke to treasure their male friends for their conversation, their loyalty, and their affection. Friendships with men are different; their minds work in another way. They're likely to be well-informed about subjects we find interesting, and though these men are just "friends" there is still a sexual frisson between us simply because they are "other." They remind us that we are women.

Still, as raging hormones quiet down during midlife, friendships with men become simpler and more enjoyable. During our twenties, thirties, and forties our friendships with men are often colored by sexual energy that makes us keep them at arm's length. We can become more companionable now. "With men, it was always very complicated, partly because of the sexual stuff going on," says Marion, who has been married for seventeen years. "I'm doing better at having male friends now, finding nice ways to connect and like each other without going to bed together."

Friendships with men give us an alternate, and sometimes unexpected, point of view. When my husband left, every one of my male friends had his number. To a man, they said, "There has to be another woman; men don't leave to be by themselves." With one expection, my women friends, like me, believed his story that he "just needed

time to himself."

It seems obvious that another woman can understand us better than a man. Why, then, do men as well as women turn to women when they want to talk on a deep, personal level? Shelley E. Taylor, Ph.D., professor of psychology at UCLA and author of *The Tending Instinct*, explains, "Women are everybody's nurturers—men, children, and each other. The evidence suggests that when women respond to someone going through a stressful event, they say, 'That's awful, I'm sorry.' They are more empathetic; men are more about advice giving."

Research done by Dr. Taylor and her colleagues at UCLA suggests that our need for friendship may be hardwired, that men and women have different neuroendocrine and hormonal responses to stress. The model for the well-known fight-or-flight response to stress was developed through years of laboratory studies with—you guessed it—men.

Women may react in another pattern, one these researchers call "tend and befriend" (hence the name for Dr. Taylor's study whose results flew all over the Internet a year or so ago). Simply put, we release the hormone oxytocin as part of the stress response. Oxytocin counters stress, produces a calming effect, and dampens the fight-or-flight response. (It's also involved in attachment between mothers and infants.)

What's more, says Dr. Taylor, estrogen enhances the effects of oxytocin, while male hormones, like testosterone, inhibit it. She continues, "A similar hormone, vasopressin, seems to be more important in men. It's related to territoriality, guarding, and patrolling." Intriguing, isn't it? Maybe that's the root of men's so-called "boundary issues" in relationships.

The female chemical reaction to stress probably evolved to protect offspring and to foster connection with social groups, especially networks of women. Our contemporary behavior is likely a continuation of those ancient patterns. Dr. Taylor and her coauthors wrote in their study, "Both men and women experience these stress-regulatory benefits of social support, but women disproportionately seek such contact, and the stress-reducing benefits are more consistent when the support provider is female rather than male." Put another way, Dr. Taylor offers, "After a while, women figure out that they will get the support they most appreciate from other women."

In addition, we've got the software to go with the hardware. Girls are taught to be thoughtful and aware of others' feelings and needs, to listen, to give, and to see things from the other person's point of view. We also appreciate that friendships take work. "Especially as I've gotten older, I have a hard time understanding people who don't make an effort for their friends," says Lola. "How can you think that friendship is something you drop in and out of? I can accept that just because you were friends with someone at twenty-three, it doesn't mean you can or should be friends at fifty. But if a friendship is important to you, it deserves good attention."

growing older and deeper

One of the pluses of getting older is that we have more time to pay what Lola calls "good attention" to our friends. When the kids are small, it may be impossible to have lunch, spend an evening, or even have a long phone conversation with a friend. During our fifties, however, changing circumstances give us new opportunities. "One of the reasons I retired is to spend more time with friends," says Alice, who had been an attorney. "Now, everybody is freer to get together."

While friends may be especially important for single women without children, those of us with families also sorely need our friends as our kids move away, or we realize that we may not live happily ever after with our husbands. Far more than men, women end up alone. Because we live, on average, seven years longer than men and we also tend to marry men older than we are, seven out of ten baby boomer women will outlive their husbands, and many of us will be widows for fifteen to twenty years. According to the U.S. Agency on Aging, nearly 80 percent of all older persons living alone are women, and it's a "growing phenomenon." Furthermore, when a spouse dies, women don't suffer the same risk of death as men, presumably because of our larger social networks. Our tendency and capacity to commit to others may, quite literally, help us survive.

Numerous studies show that social contact helps both men and women stay healthier. George Vaillant, M.D., wrote in *Aging Well*, "It is not the bad things that happen to us that doom us; it is the good people who happen to us at any age that facilitate enjoyable old age."

According to Dr. Taylor, people with support networks have "younger" stress systems, and those without show signs of accelerated aging. "We all have at least two systems that get active in response to stress," she explains. "The sympathetic nervous system regulates heart rate and blood pressure; the HPA [hypothalamic-pituitary-adrenocortical system] axis regulates cortisol and other hormonal responses. Over time, with repeated stress, these systems show signs of wear and tear; they become sluggish, or elevated, or need to be reset. This kind of damage accumulates, so older people have worse cortisol responses, or higher blood pressure, for example. But if you have social support, your responses are likely to be lower going into stress. Your baseline levels are lower, you don't react as much, and you're more likely to recover faster. You don't experience as much wear and tear, and you don't have those signs of aging." So people with good support systems are better protected against chronic diseases, including cancer, heart disease, and stroke; they also live longer.

Part of what gets us through aging is knowing our friends will be making the journey with us. Marlene, who was divorced years ago, fantasizes with her friends. "We envision a time when a few of us are pooling our Social Security checks, or we talk about getting the house by the water or in the woods and how we'll take care of each other. Sometimes we think we'll build individual cabins that are environmentally cool, and perfect for one or two people, along with a bigger house that's got the kitchen, the dining room, the library, the laundry, the TV, and the garden."

In a society where youth is everything, hanging out with friends eases our distress when we feel marginalized or "invisible." In *The Pull of the Moon*, Elizabeth Berg's middle-aged heroine says to her husband, "Have you ever sat by a group of older women out together at a restaurant, Martin, who are so obviously enjoying each other, who seem so oblivious to what used to weigh down so heavily on them? All of them wearing glasses to look at the menu, all ordering for themselves and then checking to see what the rest got. It is a formidable camaraderie I've seen among older women."

Sharing our experiences is helpful. Over the last twenty-five years, Dorothy has gone to a summer training camp for women who do martial arts. "There are a lot of gray heads in the organization now. We talk about how we're handling aging—here's what I do to keep my bones strong, here's what I do to stay flexible."

As we get older, though, it becomes harder to make new friends. Frequently, we've settled into a routine where there aren't a lot of opportunities to meet people. We may have been at the same job for a long time, and our children are no longer in school. And, unfortunately, we may just be too busy. Joanne says, "It's one of the things that trouble me, that I haven't made new friends."

Still, we tend to focus on old friendships and realize how important old friends are—friends we've had since college or made during our marriages or our working lives. During our fifties we may be impelled to look up people who knew us "when," those who knew us in high school or knew our siblings and our parents. As aging parents, aunts, and uncles die, those people who still share our memories become more precious. After years of no contact, we may try to reconnect. Thanks to the Internet, I recently tracked down one of my close girlfriends from high school. We caught up via phone and e-mail, and then got the chance to meet in person when she brought her daughter to New York on a college tour. We recognized each other from blocks away and clicked instantly. She remembered things I had long since forgotten, like the summer evening we were caught by her mother making out with two boys in her backyard. It was like seeing old black-and-white photos turn into living color.

With old friends like these, it almost doesn't matter how often we see them, because we connect so strongly when we do. "I'm in touch with a friend I met in kindergarten; she's my oldest friend," says Sarah. We hardly ever see each other, and there were many years when we didn't see each other at all. But she's a deep friend."

If we're lucky (or persistent), we've stayed in touch with old friends. We've seen each other through good times and bad, sometimes both at once. "I have my old childhood and high school friends," says Joanne. "We always get together for our decade birthdays. When we met to celebrate our fiftieth birthdays, our hostess had just had a mastectomy. You don't get to be fifty without something hard to deal with happening to you. We had a lot to talk about."

By now, life crises have leveled the playing field, bringing even close friends to a deeper level of intimacy. "We've all gone through something," says Stephanie. "Besides the good things, like bar mitzvahs and weddings, people have had cancer, have gotten divorced. And people have died."

At this age, we're meeting as grown-ups; we know who we are and we can dispense with childish things. "When I was younger, I needed my friends to define who I was. That's not true anymore," says Joanne. We've all learned that none of us is perfect. Chances are, we've seen each other naked, literally or metaphorically, so who cares about the gray roots of our hair or the messy kitchen? We focus on what's real. Most important is that we've been there for each other, we've shared the highs and the lows, and we will continue to do so.

changing friendships, ending friendships

Just as we come to terms with our parents, our spouses, our careers, and our children, we also sort through friendships during our fifties, identifying our most enduring friends and pulling away from others.

As we get older, our friendships are no longer based on the same things. "I'm seeing how individual all my women friends are," says Lola. "When the kids were little, and so many friendships came through them or were about them, my friends and I were on the same page. Now that the kids have left, what originally made us terrifically close is gone in some cases."

Of course, "being a friend" means different things to different women. By now, we may have learned and accepted what the limits of a particular relationship are. Adds Stephanie, "I've figured out that if I want to talk about certain things, I call certain people."

We've also gained a deeper understanding of what is going on beneath the surface of some relationships. As we grow older, we are usually able to see our relationships more clearly, particularly those where we have been treated badly or exploited. We may register the hurt or neglect and decide to do nothing but keep a guarded awareness. Stephanie explains, "I have a friend who makes dates and breaks them, she tells little white lies, she's always overextended. After she did this a bunch of times, I said to myself, 'Okay, this is just how she is; she's not going to change,' and I adapted to it. There are some people I'm so close to that if this were going on I'd have to deal with it. But I pick my battles differently now. I didn't want to spend my energy on that."

Or we may decide to do something. Jill, a widow who has a wide circle of friends, realized she was seldom invited to their parties. She countered by giving a festive party herself and inviting them all. Those who invited her back, she continued to see. The others she quietly dropped.

It's more difficult to directly confront friends we feel have hurt us. For example, Rachel has a hard time expressing anger with women friends. "I'm more able to get angry with men than I am with women. With women, I don't know if I have less cause for anger, or if I'm more afraid to show anger, but I hold back, or try to find a nice way to say things." We have a hard time being direct when ugly feelings of competition, envy, and anger arise. Do we imagine, on some level, that the perfect friendship between women shouldn't involve conflict, because it's *not nice* to disagree?

"It isn't that the women don't have competitive feelings, only that they have much more difficulty in acknowledging them, therefore in acting on them," writes Dr. Rubin in *Just Friends*. " . . . Indeed, it's precisely because women have, for so long, been constrained from expressing their competitive strivings cleanly and clearly that they can become distorted into the kind of petty rivalries, jealousy, and envy that sometimes infect their relationships with each other." Unspoken hurts take their toll, though, and distance grows between us.

When we don't confront the issue we may simply allow relationships to disappear. Marsha can only guess at what happened between her and a close friend she'd known since she was sixteen. "Two years ago, she bailed out. There wasn't any incident, but I think she felt envious of me. I had lost forty pounds, but she, who had always been very beautiful, had gained a lot of weight. And my book was very successful. I tried to talk to her, told her I miss her, asked her what's wrong. But she isn't responsive and is elusive. It's been devastating."

Some women find confrontation so difficult they agree to avoid it and manage to keep the relationship alive. After her divorce, Bonnie and her friend of fifteen years argued. "She kept telling me that we should never have been together, it was a terrible marriage, implying that I had wasted years of my life. I asked her to stop saying it, and she kept going. We didn't speak for about a month. We never really talked it through but decided to make up by just forgetting about it. We went out, were on best behavior, and sort of agreed not to disagree. It took a while, but things are okay again."

Annie's relationship with an old friend hasn't ended, but it certainly has changed. "Our relationship has suffered since she became a parent. For many reasons, I feel like she's doing a terrible job with her kid. All

I can think about is how critical I feel of her parenting. Because it's been almost impossible to be honest with her, I've withdrawn a lot. But I feel like a terrible friend because I can't confront her about these things."

On the other hand, a little distance can be a good thing. Stephanie says, "My best friend and I have had some tough patches. She's very self-assured and confident. I get hooked—I've had to struggle at being able to hold my own with her. There was a way I was dependent that was not totally good for me. Last year, she got involved with someone I just don't like. I realized it was an opportunity to become less dependent on her. We disengaged a little, and it's been better."

Confronting problems may allow a friendship to grow and accommodate new needs. Certainly, some women know how to work through anger and hurt. "With my best friend, I've been able to get through some very tough situations," says Noreen. "We don't fight; but when we're upset with each other, we talk about it and figure it out. It's so important to be able to express anger and upset, and walk away okay."

During a time when we're evaluating everything in our lives, we may decide to weed out some unsatisfying relationships. Sometimes, friends don't come through for us in a crisis. Sadly, we may realize that people we thought we were close to have just been fair-weather friends. "I had a lot of friends through work," recalls Diana. "But when I lost my job and my power, they were nowhere to be found—gone, gone, gone."

When we choose to end a friendship, it can be especially wrenching. Elizabeth and Isabella met thirty-seven years ago. Their friendship survived many ups and downs, including major arguments and long periods of not speaking. But in their mid-fifties, the friendship no longer worked for Elizabeth, who says, "We met when we were both young and pretty crazy. I still love her, and I have more fun with her than anyone else. But what has always driven me nuts about her has finally become too difficult and too painful. Besides, she won't accept that she plays a part in our problems. I just don't have the patience any more. I had to disengage." Elizabeth ended the relationship, but she's been in turmoil ever since. "I feel such regret and shame for having done it, even though I knew I had to," she says. "It involved breaking one of my important personal taboos: Never be disloyal to a friend. I'm still friends with my best friend from junior high, from high school. Isabella was my best friend from college. So it colored the way I think about myself. I'm someone who keeps my friends, who thinks friendships are really important, so how could I do this?" So intense are her feelings, she refers to it as her "divorce."

Friends can inflict terrible pain; they can also be an astonishing gift. Our friends sustain us through the good and the bad. We offer each other understanding, caring, and empathy. In a crisis, or when we just need to find some clarity, we go to a friend. And sometimes, it's as simple as the message one of my closest friends left on my machine: "Call me when you get a chance. I just want to talk."

TAKING STOCK AND MOVING FORWARD

✍ Think about your five closest friends. When did you last speak with them? When did you last initiate a meeting? Have you ever told them how much they mean to you? Imagine you are in your eighties. Are these the friends you want to have around you? Are there others?

∞ List other friends you see from time to time. How do you feel after you see or speak to them? Are there people you'd like to see more often? How can you make that happen?

∞ Do you have any friends you feel drain your energy, friends you'd like to see less frequently or stop seeing altogether?

∞ Do you have any male friends? If not, can you bring male friends into your life?

∞ Are there old friends you wonder about, friends you'd like to make contact with again? The alumni association at your college may be able to help you track down your roommate or other friends from college. You may also find them on the Internet.

∞ Are you a "good friend" to your friends? What can you do to be a better friend?

CHAPTER 9

the
sandwich generation
coping with aging parents

> *"My mother almost died a few months ago; she even had last rites.*
> *I realized, maybe at the time of a parent's death, those of us*
> *who've felt slighted or abused, maybe when we're ready to lose*
> *them and not be children anymore—once they're gone you're no*
> *longer a child—maybe then something clicks, and you're able to*
> *look at them in a way that you've never been able to before. But*
> *how do you do that before they're at death's door?"*
>
> —Judith, age 56

NO MATTER HOW OFTEN we read about it in newspapers and magazines, or hear it discussed on TV and radio, nothing really prepares us for our parents' aging. Unless our parents have already died, most of us will face challenging emotional, financial, and physical demands as they live the last years of their lives.

This is a much larger concern for us than it was for our parents because *their* parents tended to die at younger ages. I had only one living grandparent by the time I was eleven years old; at ages eighteen and twenty-five, my daughters have all four. Advances in medical technology and better health and nutrition have lengthened the life span. My maternal grandmother died of heart disease in her seventies; today she would have been a prime candidate for coronary bypass surgery, and would probably have lived much longer.

The demographics are dramatic. Around 1900, among couples in their fifties, only one couple in ten had two or more surviving parents. Today, it's nearly one in two. At the same time, the proportion of middle-aged couples who have at least one living parent climbed from 48 percent to 86 percent. Our relationships with our parents now typically last fifty years or more. For many of those years, we are both children and parents. We've become the "sandwich generation" or the "generational bridge." Stretched between our parents and our children, we are often called upon to help out our parents while we still have significant child-rearing responsibilities. If we're married, we may be coping with two sets of elderly parents or two elderly widows at the same time.

As fifty-somethings, we're often pulled apart by our responsibilities. About two years ago my father had a "small" stroke. The same week, one of my daughters underwent a colonoscopy for a potentially serious health problem. All the while, I was in the thick of divorce mediation—triple anxiety just when I needed to focus on work! And, of course, as background noise, there were hot flashes, night sweats, and insomnia.

Even when our parents remain healthy, our relationships with them change. It is always hard to watch their diminishment. "I hate to see how much they've slowed down and to be reminded that they're not going to be around forever," says Natalie. "Now I'm grateful for every day that they're here."

Gradually, the balance of power changes. After years of being dependent children, we may have gone through a period—if we were fortunate—when we and our parents regarded each other as peers providing mutual support. Lola was one of the lucky ones. "When we came back to town after living out West for fourteen years, my mom said, 'I don't feel as if my daughter is back, I feel as if a very good friend is back in town after a while,' and that's how it felt to me, too."

But the scales tip as we and our parents get older. They may begin to depend on us, and it's hard for all concerned. Lynette has had to help her mother out financially, and it's strained her resources. "She just needs more than I can give her," she says. "In August, I bought her an air-conditioning unit because it was sweltering. One hot day, she was sitting outside and I asked her why she didn't turn on the AC. She said, 'I can't afford to pay the bill and I can't ask you for a dollar.' It made me feel terrible. I told her I would pay her electric bills. But then she called to say Medicaid wouldn't pay for her medication, so I gave her a hundred dollars. It's a bottomless pit. I can't keep up." Even when our parents have enough money, things get touchy if they are unable to handle their affairs and we have to take over their finances, pay their bills, or manage their investments.

When one parent loses the other, the children are often the chief grief counselors. After her mom died, Lola found her father became much more dependent. Although he still lives on his own, he needs her more now and looks to her for constant support. She calls him every morning and finds it difficult to get off the phone. "I know he sits down in the morning and thinks up things to say to me. I'm sure there are days I'm the only person he talks to. He and Mom were so close. He'll never get over losing her."

We hear a lot about "reverse parenting," how we become parents to our parents. It feels peculiar, Lola says, when she has to get parental.

"I get kind of bossy. I tell my father to drink plenty of water, or I tell him to be sure to wash those pants." But reverse parenting is not really an apt description. The relationship may feel upside down, but our parents are never our children. As Natalie says, "With children you can pick them up and insist that they do thus and so; with parents you can't."

How we fare with our parents depends on how they are coping with aging. Elderly people are obviously more content with their lives when they're in good health. My mother has nothing life threatening; however, she has a host of chronic ailments, including diabetes, arthritis, macular degeneration, and a neurological condition that causes constant pain. She's miserable, and so am I, because I'm helpless to do much for her. "Aging parents force their children to admit they have limitations, that they can't do everything," writes psychologist Mary Pipher in *Another Country*. "Adult children don't have the money, the time, the living situations, the psychological sophistication, or the medical knowledge to handle things perfectly. In the end, they can't do enough. They can never repay parents for the gift of life. They can't save their parents from pain, sadness, and ultimately from their deaths."

We also need to understand what our parents are going through psychologically. Erik Erikson, one of the most influential and seminal thinkers in the field of human development, proposed that the developmental task we face during late adulthood is to develop "ego integrity," or a basic acceptance of our life as having been inevitable, appropriate, and meaningful. Failing that, we lapse into despair.

It's hard to be around parents who are disappointed with their lives. "My mother has continual regrets about what she did or didn't do," says Rachel, "and regrets about the ways that we've turned out. She is so full of regret it makes me feel very sorry for her, and also angry."

On the other hand, Lola's mother told her, years before she died, that her life had been everything she wanted it to be. She didn't want to die, but she was ready, and would have no regrets when the time came. "It was such a gift," recalls Lola.

Other psychologists have talked about a process called a "life review." Recently, my mother has tried to talk with me about what kind of a mom she was. It's led us to remember a lot that happened—good and bad. She's also worried about how I'm going to think of her; at the end of one visit, she said, "Please remember me fondly." Of course, I assured her I would.

Parents with Alzheimer's disease pose an especially poignant problem. Watching the slow, heartbreaking progression to vacancy and death is torturous. Joanne was close to her father, especially when he outlived her mother by several years. Until his eighties he was an avid hiker and a vibrant, fun-loving man. Like so many with this horrible illness, he ended his days in a nursing home. "Before he died, we lost him as a person. His physical health was good, but his ability to remember anything for more than two minutes—including who we were—was gone. Fortunately for him, a lot of that time he didn't know what he had lost."

coming to terms

While some parents provide us with emotional support and friendship, others are a constant source of anguish and stress. In a study of adult children, sociologist Debra Umberson, Ph.D., at the University of Texas, found that strain in the relationship with a mother or father increases depression. Those of us with difficult parents aren't surprised by her findings. How many of us, I wonder, relate to Jonathan Franzen's description of a visit "back home," in *The Corrections*: "On her second day in St. Jude, as on the second day of every visit, she woke up angry. The anger was an autonomous neurochemical event; no stopping it. At breakfast she was tortured by every word her mother said." One friend of mine reports that within fifteen minutes of walking into her parents' house, they are already driving her crazy.

Whatever the nature of our relationships with our parents, we try to come to terms with them now. Especially if we are parents ourselves, we can see our parents more sympathetically from another, more adult, perspective. Gail, who, at age sixteen, lost her mother, says, "I envy everyone who still has a mother. I would give anything to have known my mother as an adult."

If our parents have been difficult, we may at last be able to lower our expectations and stop being disappointed. Louisa went through a period when she didn't speak to her parents. Now, she says, "our relationship doesn't go too much beyond being superficial, but it's civil. It's not what I would want for a relationship, but I've accepted that this is what it's going to be. I cope with them better."

Like Louisa, many of us have, by now, learned how to handle our parents. We know that to avert an argument we should get off the phone when we hear a certain tone in their voice. Or we recognize other patterns and try to tailor our responses to avoid fireworks. Amanda's father is considering marriage, but he's sending out mixed messages. She says, "It's so typical. He's ambivalent about it, so he presented it sort of off-the-cuff. Then, he was angry because I didn't tell him how great the news was. But he had also said recently that he doesn't want to get married, and called it 'the *M* word.' I've learned with him: Don't get on his bandwagon too quickly because he might jump off. I explained to him, 'Sometimes you change your mind about things. Are you asking me or telling me? If I tell you it's a great idea, does that push you? And if I say it's bad, does that make you mad?'"

Sometimes it's easier to leave old baggage alone. When she divorced years ago, Rachel's father hurt her deeply. "He said he thought of my husband more as a son than me as a daughter. It was pretty devastating to hear, and it put a wedge between us that is still there." She chose not to discuss it, even when her father was dying. "Bringing it up wouldn't have helped either of us," she says, "and it would have made his last days worse."

In contrast, Marlene chose to confront her mother about some childhood events. "I had gradually put things together in my mind, and I suspected that something weird might have happened to me with an uncle who lived upstairs. I asked my mother about it and she told me, 'Yes, something did happen.' I'd been sexually abused by this uncle. She never told my father. I was furious with her; she'd seen me struggle all these years and never thought to tell me about it." The confrontation was healing, though, and Marlene now considers her mother one of her closest friends.

Sometimes, new issues arise, completely changing the color of our memories. "I found out this summer that my mother has been addicted to barbiturates for thirty years," says Gloria. "No one knew. I go through my life trying to be as awake and aware as I possibly can and to experience things, to be open to what's going on. When I think that for all these years, she hasn't been all there . . . !"

The hardest task of all, though, is coming to terms with something we learn after our parents die. The day after her father died (her mother was already dead), Alice was overcome with depression and found herself hiding in a closet. "I sat there for five hours, shaking. All I wanted to do was kill myself, and all I could do was think about how to do it." She had never felt suicidal or so "crazy" before. "I called my therapist and told him I had someplace terrible to explore and I didn't know where it would lead," she says. With her doctor, she recalled years of sexual abuse by both parents, and the bottom of her life fell out. "I used to think my mother and father were the best parents anybody ever had. Everybody said so. My siblings still say it. We were the lovely family in the Christmas pictures, the whole thing. But it was all advertising and fancy fraud." Reconciling herself to this new information does not include pardoning her parents. "Don't talk to me about forgiveness. I don't feel it's my job. If they're frying in hell, let them deal with the powers that are there, whatever they are."

making peace with our mothers

While we were growing up, many of us didn't know our fathers very well because they were often out at work, while our mothers typically stayed at home. As we matured, most of us became closer to them, but by the time we are in our fifties, our relationships with our mothers take center stage. To some extent, it's a function of statistics, since men die earlier and many of our mothers are alone.

It's also true that our relationships with our mothers are more complicated. Whether we emulate them or strive to be as different as we can, they are still the yardstick by which we measure ourselves. Mothers may become less central if and when we become parents, yet they still figure strongly. As psychologist Ruthellen Josselson, Ph.D., wrote in *Revising Herself*, "Whatever a woman is, in a deep psychological stratum of her being, either pays homage to or disavows her mother."

During midlife, while acknowledging our permanent mother-daughter connection, we often want to disengage and defuse its power. We want our mothers to accept us for who we are, rather than who they wanted us to be. And we find that they perhaps have more to offer than we thought.

For years, I carried my mother's voice in my head. I heard her when I shopped for clothing, approving of the red sweater, telling me to put the green one back on the rack. "It makes your skin look green," she'd say. I tormented myself with the spotless standards of cleanliness I remembered from my childhood. Gradually, though, I became less dependent on my mother's approval, real as well as imagined, and developed my own standards. My house is clean, but I don't mop up the bathroom floor every time I take a shower. On the other hand, I've finally allowed myself to acknowledge that my mother was sometimes right: I do look better in red.

Having children may open a new window into our mothers' behavior. As a very private teenager, I hated it when my mother said, "I can tell by the look in your eyes that something is wrong." Now that I have daughters, I know exactly what she meant.

Seeing our mothers interact with our own children can evoke powerful memories. One day, when her daughter was very upset and moaning in a melodramatic adolescent fashion that she wanted to kill herself, Amanda overheard her mother say in a scathing tone, "That's ridiculous!" "I had this flash: This was the tone of voice she'd use with us. The voice that made us feel hurt and ashamed, or that our feelings were invalid. I'm getting a new view of what it was like to grow up with her."

When we observe our children and mothers together, we sometimes recognize similarities we'd rather not see. Amanda continues, "I'd notice certain things she does and a bell would go off in my head—ding, ding, ding—because I do them, too. And I'd think, whoa, I don't like that; I want to be more aware."

At the same time, when her mother was in the hospital, Amanda saw a side she hadn't glimpsed before. "I was really impressed by her strength. The people, young and old, the aides, were totally devoted to her. As self-absorbed as she can be, she knew everybody's story.

There are things I don't like about myself that I get from her. But she also has skill and talent and an interest in other people that's admirable. And maybe I've got some of that, too."

As middle-aged adults, a new perspective shrinks our mothers to a more human size and helps us forgive them, or at least take a more balanced view. "I've reconciled myself with my mother," says Annie. "We have totally different personalities. I see now that what I took for disinterest as a child is more that she's quite shy. I was very verbal—I was the alien child, and she didn't know what to do with me."

In the past century, our generation is the one that has made the greatest departure in lifestyle from that of their mothers. Thanks in large part to the women's movement, many of us chose not to emulate our mothers. For example, when questioned in 1990, only 28 percent of the women in the Radcliffe class of 1969 saw their mothers as role models. Many were critical of their mothers for not taking risks or using their talents, or for subjugating their needs to others. More than twice as many women saw their fathers, rather than their mothers, as clear role models.

In fact, our fathers may have been the ones who helped us pursue careers. Marlene, who comes from a close-knit Catholic family, says her father was very progressive for his age and background. "My leaving town was a big coup. My mother wanted me to stay and go to the local Catholic college. Dad was my champion and got me out."

Because we lead very different lives than our mothers did, the potential for misunderstanding is greater. They often feel conflicted about us, especially if they were homemakers. On one hand, they may be happy for us and proud of our flourishing careers. Having raised successful daughters may help them feel better about themselves, and they may bask in our "reflected glory." On the other hand, they may compare themselves to us unfavorably. Our different lives may feel threatening or trigger regrets about their own missed opportunities. In addition, they may disapprove of the way we live and resent that we didn't stick to the traditional ways. My mother has always been unhappy because I moved to another state, and I wasn't the kind of daughter who came for dinner with my family every Sunday, like she did with her mom.

Nonetheless, it's likely that our mothers will be our role models for aging. We take encouragement from a mom who is aging well, and today, seventy-somethings who watch their diet and exercise regularly often look and feel much younger, even bloom. After going on antidepressants, Diana's mother is a new woman. "She's in relatively good health, for eighty-four. She's developed a social life, she has interests, she has friends, she has men that take her out to dinner, she's on the computer e-mailing me. It's phenomenal."

In contrast, some mothers are models for how not to age. After she lost her eyesight, Joanne's mother went rapidly downhill. "I had seen her as so strong and independent, but she didn't wage the good battle. The blindness destroyed her, there was nothing left; all her negative traits took over. She couldn't read, drive, canoe, fish, see her grandchildren, do crossword puzzles. Her world narrowed so much. She didn't have much of a life and she gave up."

When they are ill it's hard to watch them suffer. Marsha is extremely close to her mother, who is in very poor health. "My mother and I look and sound alike, so if something happens to her I feel like it's happening to me. I worry all the time, and I talk to her every day. She's also the funniest woman I ever met. My goal in life is to give my mother one laugh every day."

Those of us who don't enjoy our mothers live with a lot of guilt. Louisa's relationship with her mother is minimal. "I know she's not going to be here forever. But I can't bring myself to spend more time with her, and it makes me feel guilty. And how will I feel when she's gone? Even more guilty."

Regardless of our feelings for our mothers, their deaths loom large. "The fear of losing Mother doesn't even require having had an emotionally nourishing relationship with her in the first place," wrote Nancy Friday in *My Mother/My Self*. "Some women openly dislike their mothers, others cannot recall a gesture of warmth, a moment of closeness. It is not necessary to have loved your mother, even for her to have been there for you, for the symbiotic need to exist. Sometimes, in fact, the hardest mother-daughter relationship to face is the one that is only a wish-fulfillment fantasy."

Moreover, when a mother dies, we are vividly reminded that we, too, will die. As Hope Edelman wrote in *Motherless Daughters*, "Because a same-sex parent acts as a natural buffer zone between a child and her own mortality, as long as the mother is present, life—and not death—is the daughter's image of her future. When that barrier is removed, death feels more imminent to her, and decidedly more real." And if our mothers died young, our own aging takes on a sharp edge of uncertainty, or a gnawing insecurity. "Fifty-eight is a loaded age for me because in another couple of months I will have outlived both of my parents," says Stephanie. "It's as if I'm living on borrowed time."

Making peace with our mothers is important. Adult women who have good relationships with their mothers have better self-esteem and are less anxious and depressed. In addition, if and when we take on more responsibility for them, it's a lot easier when we get along well.

taking care

Our relationships with our parents change drastically when they are ill. This can happen very quickly if there is a medical "event," such as a stroke. "What's hard is having to step in and be responsible, making medical decisions, going with them to the doctor, staying on top of what's going on, changing doctors when it's not working," says Noreen. Right now, after a period with both parents in the ICU, she is breathing easier. Her parents are living independently, but there's still a lot to manage. Fortunately, she shares the burden with her brother and sister.

Providing day-to-day, hands-on care is becoming more common. According to "Family Caregiving in the U.S.," a national study done by the American Association for Retired Persons and the National Alliance for Caregiving, nearly a quarter of all households have at least one adult who has provided care (from household chores to physical care) for an elderly person during the previous twelve months. Although more men are becoming involved, this 1997 study found that almost three-quarters of the caregivers were women. Another researcher estimates that over half of middle-aged women between ages forty-five and forty-nine with a surviving parent can expect to provide care at some point in the future.

Why are these numbers rising so rapidly? Deborah Merrill, Ph.D., associate professor of sociology at Clark University in Massachusetts and author of *Caring for Elderly Parents*, a study based on interviews with caregivers and their families, provides one answer. "It's the aging of the population and the changes in the health care system. Families are providing more of the care that agencies used to provide. There's less being done in the hospital, and people are discharged more quickly, so families have more to do."

We're also shouldering a far more complicated burden. Dr. Merrill adds, "Because of improvements in technology, parents live much longer than they used to and with more medical complexities; they're also more frail. What children do now would have been done in hos-

pitals before. They're doing medical procedures, monitoring respira-
tors, changing colostomy bags. That's pretty difficult care."

In addition, the "Family Caregiving in the U.S." study found that
64 percent of the caregivers were employed. This creates enormous
conflict, especially for women, for whom balancing work and family
is all too familiar. "There's this terrible pull as to what you do with
your career, when aging parents take up more time than your career
can spare," says Ruth Steinberg, M.D., an obstetrician-gynecologist.
"If you are in a high-paying job, do you hire someone to do it and
then feel guilty that you're not there? And if you're not highly paid,
how can you now give up your job? Do you choose to be the caregiver and quit, knowing that you may be rehired at a lower status or
not at all? Or do you put Mom in a nursing home? It's an extraordinary dilemma." Several times, when her dad needed to be admitted to

the hospital, Lola had to cancel whole days of important meetings.
"I'm lucky—my boss has been very accommodating, and I have control over my schedule," she says.

We are rewarded for the huge amounts of time, energy, and work
we put into raising a child when we witness her healthy growth and
development. But with aging parents, no matter how much we worry
and how hard we work, the payoff is grim as we watch their inevitable
decline and death. There is one undeniable similarity, though, between caring for an aging parent and raising a child. When do we get
time for ourselves? "I've had times when my head was spinning
around and around, where I literally couldn't think straight," says
Amanda.

Because many of us live some distance from our parents, we may
not take care of them ourselves. Instead, we monitor caregivers from
afar. Even when parents are still living on their own, trying to make

sense of their medical condition and treatment from out-of-state is frustrating and worrisome. When my parents describe their doctors' visits, the information is always sketchy. How do I know what really happened? Are they asking the right questions? Do they hear the answers, or are they too confused, fearful, or in denial to listen to what their doctors say? Because both of my parents pursue a seemingly endless round of doctors' appointments, going with them is impossible. Yet, connecting with their doctors by phone is difficult.

According to an article in the *New York Times* in January 2003, there are nearly seven million Americans who are responsible for the care of an older relative or friend who lives, on average, 300 miles away. Because nature abhors a vacuum, our capitalist economy has found a way to fill that niche: geriatric care management companies. Such services aren't cheap. Nor are they regulated by the federal government or by the states. Still, since 1995, membership in the National Association of Professional Geriatric Care Managers has grown from 650 to 1,800. In an otherwise stagnant economy, managing our parents' care is a growth industry.

Sometimes, distance provides a helpful perspective. Because she lives on the West Coast, Joanne couldn't be as closely involved in managing her mother's care as her father or her sisters, who lived near her in the Midwest. "We were very concerned about her smoking," Joanne says. "She couldn't get out of bed because of her emphysema, but she'd lie in bed, smoking up a storm, blind as a bat. Visiting at Christmas, I happened to go up to her room and, sure enough, her bed was on fire. If I hadn't come in, she wouldn't have known, and whether she could have gotten out, I don't know. At that point, I said to my father, "She's got to go into the nursing home. I don't want her burning up you or herself."

When it comes to long-term care facilities, we walk a tightrope. Of course, we don't want to coerce our parents or limit their independence too soon. Still, we don't want to wait too long. "Often they want to stay in their own homes, but *you* see what's down the road and by the time they're ready to move into assisted living, they're too ill," says Dr. Steinberg. For elders who are reasonably healthy, there are options, such as adult day care or residential facilities that offer multiple levels of care, including independent and assisted living, that are a far cry from the grim nursing homes of the past. Once our parents become severely incapacitated, however, there are fewer alternatives.

When we are involved in caring for frail or sick parents, we also face financial dilemmas. Amanda turned down a job while her mother was living with her. This is not uncommon. In "The Metlife Juggling Study," a small, in-depth follow-up study of fifty-five of the caregivers in "Family Caregiving in the U.S.," a total of 40 percent of those interviewed reported that care-giving affected their ability to advance in their jobs. Besides taking more sick or vacation time, many had been forced to cut back to part-time or to quit their jobs altogether. Even if they remained full-time, they had passed up promotions or relocations, turned down assignments, or skipped new training opportunities. The study also found that caregivers, on average, lost over $600,000 in wages, Social Security, and pension benefits over their lifetimes. In addition, on average, caregivers spent more than $19,000 of their own money to help out with expenses such as rent or mortgage, home care professionals, food, transportation, and medications.

There are other prices to pay as well. Those of us who care for parents with chronic diseases have more of our own health problems than those who don't, and we have less time for our children and families. Even the best marriages are tested during such stressful periods. However, some husbands rise to the occasion. Lola has dinner with her father twice a week. "Of course, this has had a huge impact on Jim. We go to Dad's every Wednesday and he comes to us every Sunday. I can't imagine that Jim doesn't resent it. But support is one of his incredible strengths: It's not just that he doesn't complain, he's happy to do it." And when Lola is out of town, her husband still dines with her dad.

Though the women's movement has made considerable inroads in spearheading child care for working moms, there's little support for adults who care for their sick parents (or spouses or children). We need more and better day care centers, more flexible work hours, respite care, and long-term care insurance. Yes, we have the Family and Medical Leave Act, but that provides only unpaid leave, and it doesn't apply to small businesses. Until long-term care policy in this society changes, we continue to muddle through. Despite all that, often the experience is life affirming.

Emily, who is caring for her aged and ill mother at home, sees two sides of the coin. "This is something that's so important. Every day, I see who I am, who I want to be, and who I need to avoid being. It's really hard, but it's also an opportunity that not everybody gets." When Dr. Merrill interviewed caregivers a second time for her book, after many of them had lost their parents and they'd had a chance to think about what had happened, the majority were very happy that they had been caregivers, particularly those who enabled a parent to die at home. They felt they'd been able to fulfill their parents' last wishes to die with family and to live at home until the end. They were glad they'd done it.

But beyond fulfilling our parents' wishes, caring for them is deeply gratifying to many of us. We may enjoy a sense of accomplishment for taking on a tough role and managing it with compassion. It's a chance to assure ourselves that people we love are getting the best possible care, to reaffirm family bonds, and to give something back to our parents.

In addition, when we care for our parents, we have the opportunity to become closer and to get to know and love them again. Because of the months her mother spent living in her home, Amanda had a very challenging time; yet there was a positive side as well. "If your mom is with you for a day or even a week and then she leaves, you often just let issues slide. Because Mom was living with us, I chose to deal with the problems that came up. I didn't want to have certain conversations with her, but we had several. It's been difficult, but you know what? We've gotten to the other side of it and we're friends now."

When we care for our ailing parents, we may also learn more about our own families. "She's reminiscing about her childhood and about *her* mom," says Emily. "These are things I never knew before, and now I'll have them for the rest of my life."

Finally, at its best, taking care of our parents gives us a chance to say a loving good-bye.

when parents die

One way or another, the death of a parent is a significant event in our lives. If we've been fortunate, it may be the first time we've been touched by death. We struggle to make sense of it and reel from the loss. Ruth and her sisters were with their mother when she died. "I had never seen anybody die before. She died peacefully, but it was still really shocking and hard to grasp. Someone is there and then they're gone. It was impossible to take it in."

The mourning can be wrenching. When her father died, Marlene "fell apart. I'd never lost anyone really close to me. I adored him and considered him one of my best friends. He had been my advocate all my life. I couldn't put two sentences together for three months, and I was writing for a living. I couldn't really function for days."

On the other hand, if we've had a troubled relationship with a parent, we may feel disburdened—and guilty. We may also feel relief if our parent was suffering. Elizabeth, whose mother died a long, gruesome death from breast cancer, explains, "When someone's that ill, you mourn slowly, in anticipation. It's not like the death is a surprise. She had been quite difficult, not only physically, but also emotionally. When she died, I had a huge sense of relief."

If we're lucky, we help our parents have a "good" death. "My mother loved to sing," recalls Ruth. "She had all these silly songs she had taught us, so we were singing to her when she died. It was wonderful to be there with my sisters. It's one of the best things we ever experienced together."

Moreover, a parent's death forces us to face our own mortality. Says Sarah of her father's death, "The most profound thing is, I've had to face that we really die." We also feel more alone. As long as our parents are still living, writes Jungian psychoanalyst James Hollis, Ph.D., in *The Middle Passage*, "Even when the parental relationship has been troubled or distant, the parent is still symbolically present to provide an invisible psychic barrier."

After our parents die, it's clear that we are no longer anyone's child. Now, we can no longer assume that our parents will be there to help or to provide a buffer in case of emergency. We are the grown-ups, responsible for ourselves. What's more, our time is limited, and we're next in line. Still, hard as this is to accept, it can propel us to reevaluate, change, and deepen our own lives.

Taking Stock and Moving Forward

🙠 If you're caring for your parents, is there more you can do to take care of yourself so that you don't become physically and emotionally exhausted? Can you get more help from your siblings, children, or spouse? Can you get hospice help? Psychological counseling? Or just have the cleaning lady come more often?

🙠 Have you talked to your parents about their lives? Consider taping their stories for your children or siblings, or just for yourself. You'll probably find that their long-term memories are sharp, and you'll learn things you never knew.

🙠 Have you talked to your parents about your childhood? These years are your last chance.

🙠 Do you see more similarities between yourself and your mother than you used to? How do you feel about this? Can you talk to her about it?

🙠 Your parents are in the last decades of their lives; their time is limited. Can you bury old grudges, make peace, find resolution to the difficult times you've experienced? You will find relief and when they die, you won't be left with feelings of guilt.

finding meaning

religion and spirituality

"Now, in our fifties, I hear women asking 'what is it that actually nurtures me, my spirit?' It's absolutely not selfish. It comes from a true understanding that what we have to give to the world in maturity comes from our own being. When we're tired, or depleted, the quality of our giving is tired. What would it be like to live from a place and give from a place where we were wet, juicy and nurtured?"

—Joan Borysenko, Ph.D., author of *Inner Peace for Busy Women*

OUT RUNNING ONE DAY, I began thinking about the fifty-four-year-old friend-of-a-friend who had suddenly, inexplicably suffered a massive stroke. It was another in a spate of scary stories I had recently heard about acquaintances my age who had been diagnosed with heart disease, cancer, brain tumors, or other life-threatening ailments. "What a bad year it's been," I thought. And then it hit me—"D'oh!" as Homer Simpson would say—this year isn't an anomaly. My friends and I are in our fifties, and this is the reality we'll be living with from now on.

Social psychologist Bernice Neugarten, Ph.D., a renowned researcher on middle age, called this realization the "personalization of death." But we don't need researchers to tell us that during middle age we grow more introspective, evaluate our lives, and turn our thoughts to the time that remains to us.

We reach menopause. Perhaps a friend develops cancer. Maybe our parents die, leaving us on deck and next at bat. Something happens, and a warning bell goes off. Sooner or later, something causes a cosmic shudder, and we become aware that our time is finite. It needn't be a negative event, though—maybe a grandchild is born, and we recognize how much we have to be grateful for. Good or bad, something reminds us that time is passing and that the minutes of our lives are ticking away.

Sadly, some of us confront events so mind-shattering that everything we've ever believed is called into question. One beautiful autumn morning, the World Trade Center was blown away. Since that day, Americans have had to accept a world that is forever changed. We've been reminded that our lives can be shattered in an instant, and this realization makes relationships and connection very precious. Or, like Wendy, we suffer the unimaginable. Her thirty-nine-year-old daughter died of cancer. Still reeling, she says, "I have been through the worst thing that could ever happen to me." Such horrific punches leave us gasping for breath and asking one question: Why? Wendy struggles with anger, too. "I've been pissed off. I always thought of God as a female, but within a day after Cynthia died, I thought, 'No, God is a male. No female god would allow a mother to feel this pain.'"

She desperately searches for spiritual comfort. "I belong to a church, I do believe in a spiritual force, and I've chosen to believe there is an afterlife, although I wish someone could give me assurance. I can't be at peace with nothing. How can I think that she returns to dust and is just nowhere?"

Whether the cause is joyous or sorrowful, our heightened awareness of the fragility of life leaves us feeling vulnerable. We search for meaning, and we become more introspective. The need to connect with something bigger than ourselves becomes more and more important, especially for women. In a survey of baby boomers reported in *My Generation* magazine, 50 percent of the women polled, compared with only 35 percent of the men, said that having a fulfilling religious or spiritual life is essential to their well-being.

It's not surprising that this need surfaces at midlife, says Joan Borysenko, Ph.D., a former medical scientist and psychologist, and author of *Inner Peace for Busy Women*. "When we see that death is not far off, and impermanence is a reality, we face another round of questions: What truly do I believe? What's my faith stream? Where do I fit? What am I doing here in a body? And, Is there anything after the body is gone?"

Facing our own mortality has a positive side. It enables us to let go of what is superficial and to realize that satisfaction comes from within. We may decide that our lives are filled with too much clutter and that it's time to get rid of some stuff—both material and emotional. We may find certain friends are no longer on the same wavelength. We may accept our limits, recognizing that we can't do all we had planned. We cross a few items off our life list—I guess I'm not going to run a marathon or see the pyramids after all. At the same time, we may choose to focus on what really matters and set new priorities.

As we grow older, we may feel the need for more of an explanation or underpinning for our lives. Wade Clark Roof, Ph.D., chair of the department of religious studies at the University of California, Santa Barbara, says, "Particularly by their late fifties, people discover that nothing lasts; it's all temporary. This is a deeply spiritual situation. Sometimes they come to believe that the only anchor they can work out is in themselves. Others work it out in a religious community. But it's a time when a lot of people explore their own spirituality."

Our search for meaning is highly individual. And so are our answers. In my yoga class, for example, at the end of our closing meditation, my teacher says, "Give thanks to God, to Allah, to Jesus, to universal consciousness or life force, to whatever you believe in." She's not kidding; our beliefs cover a wide spectrum. When it comes to religion, what most characterizes fifty-something women is that nothing characterizes us.

For example, Marlene has been studying shamanism for three years. "I believe that our souls are in a state of evolution. I believe in past lives and reincarnation, that we come here with a syllabus and a soul team, having made agreements with one another to participate in our lessons. At this time of life, we're no longer so attached to our bodies. We know we are going to give them up, so we turn to our spiritual development."

In contrast, Ruth, a Catholic, has a very Western view. "I think in terms of here and now, not when I get to heaven or when I come back as a bug. If you want to think of God as universal consciousness, that's fine with me, I can go along with that. But along with not believing in religion, I don't believe that I exist other than in my physical being. And I don't believe anyone else does, either."

Oddly enough, despite their divergent views, both women are

thinking about similar issues: Why am I here? What do I want to do with my remaining time? And how do I want to be remembered?

our childhoods and our children

Not everyone goes through a spiritual reappraisal during midlife. Some of us remain committed to the choices we made earlier or that were made for us by our parents. Raised as a "cultural Jew," Sarah and her husband were in Israel during the Yom Kippur War in 1973. She says, "During the war, everyone had to choose one day when you didn't use your car because of the oil embargo. We were just beginning our own Jewish practice, so not driving on Shabbat was our first experiment. Gradually, we incorporated more and more rituals until we were living a Jewish life. We were following the Jewish cycle and the Jewish calendar in a more organic way than we ever could in America. It changed our lives." Today her husband is a rabbi, and she is strictly observant and deeply involved in Judaism.

Pat, a self-described "vanilla Catholic," went to parochial school from first through twelfth grade. "I've always believed in my faith. I believe, like I was taught in catechism, that things happen for a reason, whatever it is. I don't question that. I accept that I will know why when God chooses. I consider my faith a gift."

Louisa was also raised a Catholic, but rejected the church because she felt its teachings were irrational, even cruel, and many of its priests unscrupulous. "I began to pull away when I started masturbating. It's such a big, bad sin, and you have to confess it. Sometimes, the priest was a twisted soul who wanted to know all the details. I felt like I was doing something absolutely horrible, and I had all this guilt. Then I'd go home and masturbate again, so I'd have to go back to confession.

It made me feel like I was a pervert, that there was something wrong with me."

Ruth still appreciates the pageantry and symbolism of the rituals but abhors the Catholic precepts. "When I was in high school I became aware that my parents never went to communion, although they made sure my sisters and I went. Then I realized they were practicing birth control, so they couldn't receive the sacraments. Now, how dumb is that?"

Especially among fifty-something women, who experienced marked social change—the legalization of contraception and abortion, not to mention the "sexual revolution"—the policies of the Catholic Church, particularly around sexuality, divorce, abortion, contraception, and the exclusion of women priests, have been alienating. In the book *Defecting in Place*, a national study of nearly 4,000 feminist churchgoers, four out of five reported being disturbed by the authoritarian hierarchy and male-dominated liturgy and rituals of the church.

Although a Gallup survey found 67 percent of the Catholic population at large supported women priests, an entrenched, patriarchal hierarchy is the norm in many, if not most, religions. In *Defecting in Place*, 62 percent of Protestant women also reported feelings of alienation. "Women have been excluded from leadership," says Dr. Roof. "Religion has been largely controlled by men in its interpretation, symbols, and belief systems." No wonder women have felt alienated.

A case in point is Lynette, a religious woman who is deeply involved in her Baptist church. But it's not the church of her childhood. "I grew up in the Pentecostal church. The main reason I gave it up was the way they dealt with women. They'd have their business meeting and some sister would come up with a brilliant idea, but she couldn't state it; she had to tell it to some brother. And I thought, 'Hey, she has the brains to think it, she has the mouth to say it.'"

While every generation rebels to some extent against organized religion, our experience was more dramatic. Coming of age during the antiwar, civil rights, and women's movements engendered in us a mistrust of institutions. (Remember the QUESTION AUTHORITY bumper sticker?) We are especially sensitive to hypocrisy in the church. In a survey he conducted for his book, *A Generation of Seekers*, Dr. Roof found that two-thirds of all boomers reared in a religious tradition dropped out of their churches and synagogues during their early teens or twenties.

Ruth is perhaps the most critical of organized religion among my interviewees. She sees organized religion, in general, as a divisive, negative political influence in the world. "My sister has become very active in her church. She keeps saying it's comforting. I get really angry when I talk to her because the world isn't comfortable right now, and it's not comfortable because people hold on to ideas that separate them from other people. I don't care how comforting that is, it's not helping the world."

Adds Diana, "I became very rebellious. I wasn't given any real spiritual guidance—I just had to go to temple and Hebrew school. I got a heavy dose of the religious trappings from my parents, but I never understood where the God part was. They always said I couldn't date boys who weren't Jewish, so I married the first Irish guy I met."

Still, Diana says she identifies herself as a Jew, a feeling that has intensified since September 11. "It was a sea change. I now feel very Jewish and very American. Not Jewish, in a religious sense, just very connected to my Jewish ethnicity."

Many women who grew up as Jews in the aftermath of the Holocaust feel a strong desire to preserve Jewish rituals. "I wouldn't say I'm a religious person, and I never could find a congregation that really works for me, but we do Passover, we do Hanukkah, we might do Shabbat," says Stephanie. "It has meaning to me that people have been doing this stuff for three thousand years."

Though two-thirds of baby boomers dropped out of an organized religion while in their teens and twenties, Dr. Roof found in his surveys that many boomers of all persuasions returned to religious institutions when they became parents. We may not believe, but we belong, especially when it comes to important milestones, like births, marriages, and deaths.

For example, Annie made a decision to be more observant of Jewish tradition after she had children. "It wasn't till I was thirteen that I realized that Jews didn't have Christmas trees—we always had one when I was a kid. But I want my children to know they're Jewish. I've sent them to Sunday school, and we celebrate the holidays. I want them to understand the rituals and the culture and to know about anti-Semitism. If they want to believe in God, that's up to them. I don't."

Although she is a lapsed Catholic, Noreen has sent her children to the Catholic Church to accommodate her husband's wishes. "My husband is a practicing Catholic, she explains. "We looked into other religions but Frank just wasn't comfortable. I wanted the children to be part of an organized religion—I do believe in that—so I said as long as he didn't have a problem with me expressing my beliefs, I was ok with them being raised Catholic."

Lola had a strict upbringing as a Lutheran—"You had to be dead not to go to church in my family," she says—but she adopted her husband's faith when she married and had children. "My husband was categorically clear that he would never ever go to a Christian church, period. He was raised as a Quaker. I wanted the kids to have the experience of growing up in some kind of religious community, and Quakerism was fine with me."

Many of us return to our roots as we approach midlife. Laura had long been involved with yoga—intellectually, physically, and spiritually. During her late forties, when she was trying to get pregnant, she felt adrift. "I remember sitting and chanting at the end of a yoga class one day, and I thought, 'Here I am: I'm Jewish, my father and my uncle were rabbis, and I'm sitting here chanting in Sanskrit. I wonder if my own religion has anything to offer me?'" She and her husband found a synagogue they liked. "I was a rabbi's daughter and I had a very solid Jewish upbringing and education, but it was spoon-fed to me. Now I'm approaching it more thoughtfully. I never thought there was a spiritual aspect to Judaism. This synagogue is fun and lively, and there's also a very strong spiritual element—it weaves it all together."

finding many paths to god, as well as many gods

Whatever we want for our children, many of us simply cannot find a home for ourselves within organized religion. That doesn't mean, however, that we aren't deeply religious. Many of us, though, prefer to think of ourselves as spiritual rather than religious because, even in our fifties, we remain open to new ideas and rituals that connect us to the divine. In fact, according to Dr. Roof, "boomers are the carriers of the distinction between religion and spirituality in the culture." Our generation has brought the idea of a "spiritual quest" into common parlance, and our search for spiritual meaning goes beyond youthful experimentation; for many, it is a lifelong process of questioning and seeking answers. "I believe in something larger than me," says Noreen. "I believe in positive energy, the energy of prayer; and I pray, just about every day. I believe in spiritual guides. If I go to functions where people are Jewish, I take part; if I go to a Protestant church, I take part; if I go to a Catholic church, I receive communion. But I'm not a member of any organized religion. I believe God understands."

Natalie agrees. "I don't feel like I need to physically be in the church any more. But I spiritually have a connection to God and speak to him through prayers."

Suzanne continues to experiment. "I was christened a Presbyterian, grew up and became active in the Baptist church. In college I became an Episcopalian. Then I studied comparative religions and realized there was a whole lot more, so I moved to Colorado and started doing Native American stuff. When I went to Bali, I gave an offering to the gods at the chapel there. I think there are many gods, and they have different names, and they have one name, and they're all connected."

Even Sarah, who remains deeply committed to organized religion, recognizes that it's a construct for something much bigger. "The form is the particular religion that somebody chooses or doesn't choose to be connected with. If there's God, it's not that there is a Jewish God; God is one."

Our spiritual searching is far more wide-ranging than that of earlier generations because today, the opportunities to pick and choose are global. We are not tied to the religious practices of our parents or even to those of our own culture. Coupled with this is our growing consciousness that this is one world, politically and environmentally, and that we are all connected. So we improvise, borrowing freely from many traditions to develop our own dynamic religious practices.

Marlene has traveled far in her search for answers. "My quest has been for spiritual truth, not a particular form of it. There are things about Judaism I really appreciate; there are things about Buddhism I find very profound. I'm pretty eclectic, open. I feel like I have a direct connection to spirit so I don't need intermediaries, like church." She traveled to South America to learn more about shamanism, which has become an important part of her spiritual practice. "People look out at the same world and see completely different things. But the shamans believe that there is a kind of stream underneath all of it, universal and outside of time, that you can tap into. That's part of what shamanic training is. I've had that experience. I can get there; it's pretty amazing."

While some midlife women range far and wide in their spiritual quests, others find that, like Dorothy in *The Wizard of Oz*, there's no place like home and that we can find answers by tuning in more closely to what lies within us. In her workshops on women and spirituality and mind-body health with many women in their fifties, Dr. Borysenko reports, "More and more women ask, 'What would it be like to sit in meditation, to develop a practice that would allow me to go beyond dogma, simply to sit in the stillness?' They go back to their inner lives, pick up the journals that they haven't looked at in years, start to think about their dreams, and realize that here are places, beyond the fast pace of life, where they can pay attention."

searching for meaning and connection

Whether we stay in the Catholic Church, revisit our Protestant roots, do transcendental meditation, study shamanism, practice yoga, or make Judaism our own, we are all searching for meaning. Fifty years old is a real turning point. People we know and care about may have died, and with that comes the dawning realization, deep down in our bones, that we will also die. "Once you reach about fifty-five, your next big birthday is sixty, and you start to feel old, because you know the landmark after that is seventy," says Dr. Borysenko. "You realize you haven't got a lot of time left. If your true desire is to become a contemplative, it's time to leave for the forest now."

We search for answers because we sense that believing in something will give us comfort. But many women, myself included, feel as Amanda does: "I wish I believed in God or in some sort of spirituality. There's that need to be part of or believe in something outside of yourself. I know so many people are sustained by it. But I've never had a strong enough belief to find solace."

Still, even when we don't have an answer, many of us believe that we are on a journey, and that there is an unseen, unknowable force that guides our lives. It was striking that so many of the women I interviewed had reached a similar understanding, despite their different backgrounds. "I really believe that we are all put on a certain path and obstacles are thrown in the way," says Natalie, who was raised Catholic. "We either start finding out how to navigate the obstacles, or we get stuck."

Marion grew up in a Jewish home, but she felt spiritually adrift until she began to study yoga. Several years ago, she went on a weeklong retreat where she practiced yoga four hours a day. It was "transformative," she says. "It changed me and opened me up spiritually." Now a teacher as well as a student, she's learned a lot. "I believe in a spirit greater than me. It doesn't have a human form, but I believe in an energy, some presence greater than us. I don't believe there are any true accidents. Even when things are at their most difficult, there's a reason. I'm not saying it feels good, but I try to look at things and say, 'Okay, there's an opportunity for growth here.'"

Lynette's faith is concrete, and based on the everyday. She explains, "No matter how difficult I find life—and I've had times where I had one package of chicken noodle soup and two potatoes, and I made soup and fed my daughter and went into my room and bawled my eyes out—the Lord has always provided for me. I pray about everything. You should hear me pray for my basketball team. A friend told me not to waste my prayers. But I figure, if I want something, I ask God to give it to me. If God says no, it's no."

Sarah's faith is also a constant, even though it's more abstract. "Every moment, I know there is God. I choose to live my life in relationship to God. It's not like I always feel God's presence. The Jewish teaching is you get up in the morning and you say a *brakha*, a blessing. You live, saying, 'Okay, life has meaning,' whether or not you understand what it is."

Women who choose to remain in organized congregations are fortunate in having valuable support, even when their faith is shaky. Sarah has found her religious "family" to be enormously helpful during her bleakest times. "I have a temperament where I can experience things as very, very black. Since I live within a religious framework and community, I can go to a darker place because I have so much to come back to. I feel connected to other people who care about the same things I care about."

Wendy calls her church the "church I will belong to without embarrassment. These are my best women friends; I share true intimate space with them. The entire time I was on the other side of the country, my daughter dying, they called, they e-mailed, they made conference calls to visit with me. You know they're friends when you don't have to explain, they're just there."

When we don't find answers or community, the results can be distressing. "I think about those existential questions and I come up with very pessimistic thoughts," says Elizabeth. "There's suffering because there's suffering; there's no existential reason for it. Ultimately, I think there is no meaning."

Yet, accepting that there is no answer can itself be a deeply spiritual experience. Amanda explains, "My mother was really sick and I thought she was going to die. I felt like I was being tested, like Job. I kept thinking, 'Why me?' and I realized, 'Well, why the fuck not you?' Things got so bad, I felt like I was standing on the edge of a precipice. I couldn't go on and I had to go on. I can't explain it, but at some point I had to release everything and accept that there's a force bigger than me. I just had this sense of the cosmos; there are things out there we just don't understand, and we're not going to. It didn't matter whether I wanted control or not. I didn't have it. It was scary and liberating."

Wendy had a similar experience caring for her dying daughter. "There is some relief in coming to the point of knowing you don't have control. It takes some of the weight away. No matter what I do, I can't make it okay; I have to leave that in somebody's, something's, some power's hands. I choose to call it God. There was this amazing sense of wonderment. It was a sacred time. I don't know of any other way to describe the intimacy we shared. It was an absolute gift to feel such total acceptance from her, knowing that she trusted me and I was the person she wanted there."

being in the present

Even if we don't find answers that sustain us, we may have precious flashes of insight when we tune in to something bigger than we are. Back in the psychedelic 1960s, psychologist Richard Alpert, aka guru Baba Ram Dass, used to call this the experience of "be here now."

These moments come in many ways. Mine often happen when I'm in my garden. Apparently, I'm not alone. According to the National

Gardening Association, interest in gardening has surged among baby boomers. Seeing how our gardens attract birds, butterflies, and even pests, like deer and raccoons, reminds us of the interconnectedness of all life. Although I've been a gardener for a long time, my garden has provided particular solace over the past three years. I've learned humility and patience as I watch glorious fruits and vegetables grow from tiny seeds. And my amazement as I witness perennials returning to life every spring gives me a feeling of awe close to faith.

Sue, a nurse-midwife, often has this feeling when she assists at a birth. "I don't know how to explain it. When you deliver a baby with some people, there's just this amazing feeling between yourself, the baby, and the family that is not of this world. It's from some other world."

In addition, sex can be an avenue for transcendence for some women. In an exploratory survey published in 2002 by the Wellesley Centers for Women in Massachusetts, Gina Ogden, Ph.D., found that women connected during sex to "an energetic principle beyond themselves, variously named by respondents as God, Goddess, nature, creativity, a higher power, or some other term denoting life force." Interestingly, older women reported more of a relationship between sexuality and spirituality than younger ones. For example, 58 percent of respondents age sixty and older reported having "experienced God in a moment of sexual ecstasy," compared with 23 percent of those under thirty. Who says older women don't get much out of sex?

However we get there, wrote storyteller, author, and scholar on mythology and religion Joseph Campbell in *The Power of Myth*, these moments, rather than some abstract "meaning of life," are what we are searching for. "I think that what we're seeking is an experience of being alive, so that our life experiences on the purely physical plane will have resonances within our own innermost being and reality, so that we actually feel the rapture of being alive. That's what it's all finally about, and that's what these clues help us to find within ourselves."

Strangely, we may find ourselves most intensely connected to life when we are in the midst of death. Wendy recalls a day of almost surreal clarity while she was with her daughter. "It just switched. I went from worrying, 'Is she going to get better? Am I going to get home to my husband?' to 'This is my life at this very moment. She is alive and this is today.' I was living in the moment as much as I ever have in my life. We all say we have to love and appreciate each day, but we get caught up in worries. I don't know how it happened, but that day I had true gratitude that I was able to be there."

thinking about the future

Our heightened sense of the fragility of life propels us not only to reevaluate how we're living our lives now, but also to think about our legacy. "I hope I look back and feel I've done enough, that I wasn't stingy, because that's what you leave behind," says Amanda. "You want your grandchildren and people who knew you to say, 'I learned something, I got something from her, I was proud to be a friend of hers.'"

This kind of thinking is not unique to us. Erik Erikson, one of the patron saints of adult development and a pioneer in the field of psychology known for the concept of the "identity crisis," called this the midlife crisis of "generativity versus stagnation." (Erikson proposed that in each of eight stages of life, we tackle a developmental task that involves a psychological choice.) While he defined generativity as "the concern in establishing and guiding the next generation," others have since expanded his definition to mean a voluntary obligation to care for others, in the broadest sense.

As we get older, then, we may yearn to commit ourselves to something important. What used to be called the "me generation" is becoming increasingly concerned with connecting to and helping others.

Some of us find a way to do this through our religious affiliations. Joanne's grandfather was a Unitarian Universalist minister, so she was brought up in that tradition. She left the church when she was in her twenties because it seemed too "amorphous" but began to go again during her mid-fifties when she felt the urge to reconnect with a socially conscious community. Today, she devotes many hours a week to the "Units," ushering at Sunday services and working on several church committees. "I love the community because it embraces so many generations. It's a place where the cycle of birth and death is being played out. There is something wonderful about seeing young kids born into it, growing up, getting older."

Joanne describes her congregation as "a caring community, trying to address questions about economic and social justice in a religious context. How do we deal with this president and a warmongering state? What can I contribute? It gives me an opportunity for social activism, which has been missing for so long from my life," she says.

Similarly, Lynette is deeply involved in social activism through her church. "I've worked with an association of churches to help keep kids off the street. The churches pool money; there is a house for people with AIDS, a house for people with mental illness. We pay for tutoring at a couple of schools, and we have a weekend program where we drive food to people."

Many religions have traditions that include social activism. Among Jews, for example, there is "Tikkun Olam," or the healing of the world, the imperative to do something to make the world a better place. Stephanie has worked all her life as an environmental advocate. "A lot of my values came out of my Jewishness, my sense of being engaged in the world and trying to take care of the world," she says.

The same is true for Lola. "In Quakerism, everyone is equal and everyone has equal access to God. My responsibility to God has to do with making a contribution, how I conduct myself toward other people, toward the earth. I feel I have an obligation to express gratitude for what I have."

Many fifty-somethings find they want to engage in some form of social activism or other altruistic activity. Apart from religious organizations, many of us channel this need into volunteering. According to the AARP Bulletin, Americans fifty and over are volunteering at a higher rate than ever before in a wide range of community service activities. We volunteer because we want to give back.

Sue, for example, has been volunteering with Habitat for Humanity, which builds houses for low-income people. "Habitat is a great organization because it's concrete—you can really see what you're doing," she says. And Rachel, who has long been a vegetarian, has deepened her commitment by taking up the cause of animal rights.

An intriguing development among women is a new movement, Women-Business-Spirituality. One of the organizers, Barbara Littrell, president of B. Littrell Communications Corporation, former president of *Working Mother* and *Working Woman* magazines, says the idea took off as a result of 9/11, Enron, and the other corporate corruption scandals. "Women at all levels of business are hungry to find like-minded women who care about business, spirituality, ethics, and values. It's about connectedness and a respect for the individual, a recognition of diversity, as well as a real practice of trying to help people have good lives and good work. We say, 'Don't check your values at the door. Instead, nurture your own personal spirituality, so you are a balanced, centered person, knowing what your values are and being willing to speak up for them.'" The movement encompasses everything from how to do a performance appraisal or fire someone to being a whistle-blower.

Business and spirituality? Many of us would have scorned the idea when we were younger. But today we realize that there are many ways to satisfy our need to give to others as well as our desires for meaning and connection. As Annie says, "I used to think that everyone had to be an activist. Then I realized that not everyone had the temperament for it. There's lots of ways—through work, through art. Find something you love doing that involves trying to create more justice in the world."

We don't have to let the knowledge of aging and death undermine us as we get older. In fact, our increased perspective and growing awareness of our mortality can ultimately free us from the humdrum, and give our daily lives more purpose and meaning. Our fifties are the time of life when we ask ourselves: "How do I get to a place where my own well is filled, where I'm truly in touch with spirit, whatever that means to me?" In finding the answer, we enrich ourselves and our relationships to others. After all, as Sarah says, "at some point, we are all part of humanity. Am I anybody if I'm not part of humanity?"

Taking Stock and Moving Forward

∝ Developing a sensitivity to a larger life force can provide ease in coping with life's vicissitudes. Have you found a way to connect to a larger force—whether God or simply an acknowledgment of a universal energy beyond our rational selves?

∽ Notice how you feel when you are alone in nature—walking in a forest, on a beach—or when you are making love. Do you feel a sense of wonder and peace?

∽ Think about the religious tradition in which you grew up. Is it still meaningful to you? To whom or what do you turn when you have spiritual questions?

∽ Does your church, synagogue, or other group nourish your spirit? If not, can you find a religious community that will?

∽ Do you pray or meditate? Notice how you feel afterward.

∽ Are you comfortable with yourself as an ethical person? How do you want to be remembered by family, friends, colleagues? What do you want to leave behind?

∽ Do you feel the need to contribute to the world in some way? Do you do volunteer work? Contribute to charities? Mentor younger women?

it's our turn now

writing the new script

OUR FIFTIES, CERTAINLY A TIME of transition, can also be a time of transformation. As we mark significant milestones on our journey through life—our children moving on, changing relationships with friends or partners, our own aging bodies, the deaths of parents or other loved ones—we reflect and reevaluate. We need to come to terms with the past and, at the same time, we must also acknowledge the major changes going on in the present. Then, we can turn our eyes to the future.

Some of us endure periods of fear and emptiness as we figure out who we want to be and where we're going. Much depends on whether we look back through the "eyes of regret" or the "eyes of grace," says psychologist Joan Borysenko, Ph.D. "It can be a very scary time, particularly depending upon how much healing you've done, and what your spiritual life is about. A lot of women look back over their lives and say, 'If I hadn't married that low-down dirty dog . . .' or 'I waited too long to have children,' or 'I wanted to go to medical school and I believed everyone who said I couldn't, so my career doesn't nourish me.' That's a hard thing, when they stop long enough to see they don't like the choices they've made and it's too late to go back. On the other hand, they can say, 'Who I am is a result of what I've gone through, good, bad, and indifferent, and I accept it all.'"

This is especially true when we're dealt an unexpected hand. When I turned fifty, I anticipated changes in my life. My children were nearly grown and would soon be out of the house. I knew I had to figure out a new focus for the future, but I didn't expect my world to shatter, as it did when my husband left.

Similarly, within the space of a few years, Gail's husband died, she was diagnosed with breast cancer, had to declare bankruptcy, and lost her job. Any one of those blows could be enough to flatten some women. Nevertheless, she now says, "My life is pretty good." How did she get through? Certainly, she availed herself of therapy, antidepressants, and other supports to get back on her feet. But, she maintains, there was also something else: "I believe the universe will take care of us, if we let it. When things happen in our life, there's energy that we need to be open to and pay attention to. When opportunity knocks, you've got to open that door and look to see what's there."

resiliency and coping

What does it take to face aging and, at the same time, retain our sense of confidence in the future and create the lives we want? How can we be open to change and better able to meet the challenges of our fifties?

Resilience helps. Resilience is the capacity to remain elastic, to bounce back instead of breaking when we face adversity. Some of us are naturally more resilient than others. Optimists tend to adjust better to stressful events, while pessimists may be more vulnerable. It's not known whether what matters is temperament per se, or the different strategies optimists and pessimists use to cope with hardships.

In addition, some of us are more willing to take chances. Within the last three years, Marsha left her husband and her job. "I come from a family of risk takers. I was born into a chaotic situation, so comfort has never been an option. I've never been comfortable in my life. Because I've felt like I had nothing to lose, I reinvent myself all the time. This isn't the first time. I am willing to unzip my life and step out of it." (Marsha now has a beautiful apartment and a flourishing career.)

But pessimists can take heart (even though it's out of character): Biology isn't destiny. Shelley E. Taylor, Ph.D., a professor of psychology at UCLA who has studied coping in women, clarifies, "Personality isn't stamped early in life . . . there's a lot of wiggle room. The die isn't cast by the time people are six or seven years old." So even if we're pessimistic by nature, it doesn't mean we can't learn to withstand the trials and tribulations that life occasionally flings our way.

Even in adulthood, when personality is well established, we can learn to be resilient. In a series of three studies, researchers found that people drew upon previous experiences to help them with a current problem, regardless of whether it was similar to a difficulty they'd experienced before. They had built up their "coping repertoires."

Resilience is also tied to health. In the midst of crisis, taking care of ourselves may be the last thing we think about doing, but it's probably even more important than ever. In my first few months alone, I'd repeat this mantra to myself every day: "eat, sleep, exercise, vitamins, work, friends." The final word was highly significant because getting help from other people is one of the most important ways we cope.

Indeed, our relationships are critical. Scores of scientific studies show that people with a social network are happier and healthier.

From a nurturing relationship with our parents to a supportive mentor, from a good marriage to close confidants, relationships provide us with support and help when it matters most. We don't need huge numbers of relationships to benefit. It helps to be part of a social network, but, says Dr. Taylor, "what you really need is one or two close friends. As long as you have that, it doesn't matter."

Women are very likely to reach out during stressful times. An impressively consistent body of research—more than thirty scientific studies of how people cope with stress—shows that women turn to others more than men do. In addition, women more often offer support to friends, relatives, workmates, and colleagues. Noreen says of her closest friend, "It's not one-sided. She takes care of me and I take care of her. And with my other friends, it's the same way. In my friendships, it's equal."

We turn to our friends not only during times of trouble but also for companionship, which becomes even more valuable as we go through our fifties. We know our relationships will sustain us as we get old. Women are also likely to maintain strong ties to family, especially to children and grandchildren, as we age. "I'd like to be able to see my children married and having kids, from a very selfish point of view," admits Ruth. "I'm really looking forward to seeing them grow into people with families because I think it will add richness and complexity to my life."

the joys of juggling

While friends and family keep us sane, it may be that the very nature of our lives has helped us become resilient. Despite changes in their roles, men of our generation have still had a fairly straightforward script to follow. But we've had to consciously invent our lives, without clear role models. For example, I was the first person in my family to finish college, as well as the first woman to have a career. We've broken stereotypes, fashioning new garments without any patterns. Not an easy task (especially when you can't sew at all, like me).

Not only have we created our own lives, but we've also recreated them time and again, when the situation demanded. Most of us have experienced a lifetime of conflicting roles and responsibilities. As young adults, we juggled marriage and career. We interrupted our careers to have babies, then struggled to balance marriage, job, and children. In midlife, we may still be doing all of that, while also going back to school or caring for elderly parents. A friend of mine recently started babysitting for her grandchild a couple of afternoons a week because her daughter is divorcing. Get ready, because it's time to toss another ball into the air.

We've had to become adaptable to accommodate the frequent shifts, interruptions, and changes in our lives. We've learned to have contingency plans so we can respond to the unexpected. These traits are valuable as we get older. "The flexibility that women are pushed to develop when they're juggling in earlier parts of their lives comes to the surface and is part of graceful aging," says Sarah. "Also, women more often have had to face not getting what they wanted right away, making sacrifices, putting things on hold, putting themselves on hold. We know a lot about frustration, and now, handling frustration is a useful skill because aging, by definition, is filled with it."

Most of us play multiple roles at the same time—wife, mother, colleague, daughter, volunteer, chauffeur, congregation member, to name a few. "My primary role changes all the time," says Noreen. "I've been an educator for thirty years and a counselor for eighteen, now I'm also training other people. I've also been a wife for many years, and I'm the mother of two children. And I really like being a woman with my female friends." In addition, for the last six years, she's been working for her doctorate. She adds, "It all has to be woven in."

There's considerable evidence that occupying multiple roles is good for us in the long run. For example, when Cornell University sociologist Phyllis Moen, Ph.D., studied a group of women over a period of thirty years, those with more roles lived longer, healthier lives. Rather than causing overload—and of course, there are days when it feels that way—involvement in many areas actually enhances our day-to-day psychological well-being.

There's also synergy among the various roles we play; skills in one area boost our abilities in another. When Marian Ruderman, Ph.D., a research scientist at the Center for Creative Leadership in Greensboro, North Carolina, studied personal well-being and effectiveness among women managers, she found that commitment to multiple roles was beneficial. "They learned managerial skills from their personal lives. They'd say, 'If I can get along with my mother-in-law or brother-in-law, I can get along with anyone.' Or they sharpened their negotiating skills by dealing with their kids, or became strategic planners by helping their parents with long-term planning."

Managing so many disparate tasks builds self-esteem and confidence. The authors of *Women's Ways of Knowing* confirm, "Women don't learn in classrooms; they learn in relationships, by juggling life demands, by dealing with crises in families and communities." Naturally, playing multiple roles in life is a given for most of us. "When one cannot expect one's marriage to last for a lifetime or count on the continuation of one's job after a merger or a corporate buyout, the ability to respond to the opportunities that present themselves is a real advantage," adds Janet Zollinger Giele, Ph.D., a professor of sociology at Brandeis University.

Because our lives have been so fluid, we've learned to ad lib and roll with the punches. As Marsha says, "I have plans, but I also have the willingness to be surprised by things." As a result, we arrive in our fifties feeling confident and competent, with a strong sense of self. For example, now that Diana has her own advertising agency, she says, "My work is a dream; I don't have to work so hard and I can accomplish what I need to. I know exactly how to do things, I trust my instincts, I know people, and I don't second-guess myself."

In addition, we've learned to trust our own inner voices, which guide us when we are pulled in many directions, or have to choose among various (often less than ideal) alternatives. We've accumulated enough experience along the way to know that we'll cope with whatever comes along. "When you've lived enough, you've got a track record, you know you've been through things and you've done okay so far, so you know you'll do okay with whatever presents itself," says Marlene. "That's the beauty of having life experience."

"possible selves"

As we've learned to adapt to changing circumstances, we may also have become adept at envisioning what Stanford University professor of psychology Hazel Markus, Ph.D., and University of Washington professor of social work Paula Nurius, Ph.D., called "possible selves." We may have a self we want to be, a self we fear we'll become, or an ideal self. Heck, we might have a whole stable full. Drs. Markus and Nurius wrote in the journal *American Psychologist*, "The possible selves that are hoped for might include the successful self, the creative self, the rich self, the thin self, or the loved and admired self, whereas the dreaded possible selves could be the alone self, the depressed self, the incompetent self, the alcoholic self, the unemployed self, or the bag lady self."

Possible selves are ideas of ourselves that represent hopes, fears, and fantasies. They come from how we see ourselves in the past but represent the future. And they are different from, but also connected to, our current self. They may be our ideas of the selves we could become, the selves we hope we become, or the selves we fear we might become.

In a study of people who had recently experienced a life crisis, noted Drs. Markus and Nurius, those who described themselves as "recovered" differed from those who hadn't, not in their description of their current selves, but in how they saw their possible future selves. They were more likely to describe their future selves as "optimist, long-lived, helpful, lots of friends, happy, satisfied, confident, and secure," and less prone to use words like "unpopular, nonaggressive, unimportant, weak, unable to fit in, a failure, to die young, have a heart attack, become depressed, or experience a breakdown."

Imagining a positive future helps us stay open to new opportunities. At midlife, when we're reinventing our lives, our possible selves motivate us to set goals and pursue our dreams. And seeing our possible selves helps when we find ourselves in rough seas, or when the boat capsizes entirely. Imagining myself on *Oprah* helps get me through those days when I stare at the computer, my mind mush, and the words won't come.

growth through crises

John Lennon was on target when he wrote, "Life is just what happens to you while you're busy making other plans." We like to think we have control but, of course, we don't. Some of us get to our fifties relatively unscathed; others aren't as lucky. Catastrophe strikes because life is unpredictable. "It has nothing to do with being good, or hardworking, or pure of heart," says Lola. "Life can be very cruel, and conversely, people are much stronger than we think."

Responding well to a crisis builds resilience. Stephanie, who has had more than her share of pain (her mother committed suicide when she was eleven, and her husband left her after she was disabled in a car accident), says, "I've lived through such hell at different periods, physically and emotionally. I now have the sense I could live through anything if I had to." That kind of confidence is like money in the bank.

How we cope in a crisis is key to our resilience. Active coping strategies reduce stress and depression. They include problem solving, taking direct action to confront an issue, and seeking support. In fact, just feeling like we're doing something helps, while avoidance strategies, such as denial, withdrawal, or alcohol, only exacerbate problems (although I've found there's a time and a place for everything). In addition, the more we do to have some control over what happens to us, the less helpless we feel and the less vulnerable to depression we are.

Reframing a stressful event also has its benefits. Don't deny that something is happening, but look for the positive aspects. Judith and her partner had just finished expanding their day spa, when the city took the building by eminent domain. At first, they were devastated. Then, she says, "we went forward with the word 'better' in mind. We had a vision and belief that this meant we were supposed to be somewhere else, even though we didn't have the funds to move. Rather than crumple under adversity and go into victim mode, we pulled it off, with the help of a loan from a community bank. We had faith and a belief that it's in the breakdowns that the breakthroughs happen, that a crisis is a crisis-opportunity. It's spirit." Today they have a spanking new, bigger spa in a beautifully restored Victorian house.

Counting our blessings is another way to reinterpret an event. Gail was reeling when, after a string of shattering events, she lost her job. The date was September 10, 2001. "The next morning I was feeling angry and weepy. The TV was on and suddenly I saw a plane fly into the World Trade Center. I realized, who the hell am I to worry about losing my job when this is happening? It put things in perspective for me."

Whatever name you give it—making lemonade from lemons, shifting our perspective—reinterpretation is helpful. "In some cases people will say, 'Losing my job was the best thing that ever happened to me,' or women with breast cancer will say, 'Now I make sure I talk with my daughter every other day' or 'I have lunch with a friend once a week,'" says Dr. Taylor. "They shift to areas of life where they can make changes that are positive."

In the aftermath of misfortune and trauma, we are changed people. We think of trauma as rape, war, incest, and other, usually violent, events. But serious disease, being left by your husband, and financial reversal are all trauma, which is defined as "a startling experience which has a lasting effect on mental life; a shock." A traumatic event shatters our assumptions, changes how we think about the world, and makes us feel helpless. Our recovery from trauma involves trying to understand why it happened, restoring our self-esteem, and coming up with a new sense of meaning for our lives.

Rebounding from a trauma is not without benefits. In her paper "Relational Resilience," psychologist Judith V. Jordan, Ph.D., notes, " . . . Working through trauma and severe stress can in fact lead to a deepening appreciation of the preciousness of life, a wisdom that eludes those who maintain illusions about their own invulnerability; it also creates an abiding respect for the power of human connection accompanied by an increasing awareness of our absolute need for the love and support of others."

Catastrophes build our resilience in many ways. They solidify our relationships with friends and family. In the aftermath of my divorce, I marveled at how many friends I had and how deep some of these relationships were. Knowing we have people we can count on is another large deposit in the resilience bank.

We may even come to believe that, horrible as it was in the short term, a terrible crisis was the best thing that ever happened to us. "Some of the hardest things that happened in my life were the most growth producing," says Marlene. "So I try not to make judgments anymore about things. I have come around spiritually to: It's all good."

In some instances, we actually come to thrive in the aftermath of grave misfortune. In *Personal History*, Katharine Graham's autobiography, she describes herself when she was forced to take over the *Washington Post* after her husband's suicide: "What I essentially did was to put one foot in front of the other, shut my eyes, and step off the edge. The surprise was that I landed on my feet." Ms. Graham became one of the most powerful women in the country. In her nearly thirty-five years at the *Post*, she transformed it into a national, high-caliber newspaper and showed enormous skill and courage in handling both the Pentagon papers and Watergate. Thousands, including many world leaders and celebrities, flocked to her funeral.

taking charge
and moving forward

So, we've made it to our fifties. We've probably accumulated some bumps or bruises along the way, but the twists and turns of our complicated lives have taught us a lot about flexibility and making choices. If we've had to deal with excruciating issues—divorce or widowhood, a child with a chronic illness, our own struggle with breast cancer or disability—we've learned that even when we have less control than we'd like, we're resilient enough to survive the unexpected.

In many ways, we've come to terms with who we are, and we're in our prime—like Stephanie, who says, "What I couldn't see at twenty-five was that, okay, I've been a good person, I've been a mensch in the way I've treated other people. I've managed to be productive in the world, be a good parent, be a good friend, heal, do all those things, under pretty hard circumstances, and so I have a certain appreciation for my own strength now. It's like, oh yeah, I'm not chopped liver. It's not just that I survived, but that I'm still cooking on all burners, more or less . . . Well, maybe the pilot light is kind of dimming, a little. But even though there have been a lot of things in my life that I wish hadn't happened, I feel like I own my life, and I embrace it."

Both self-acceptance and accepting change are important to our well-being as we age. Amanda explains, "I think aging gracefully means accepting whatever the next stages are and finding the happiness, the good, and satisfaction in what those bring, as opposed to pining for something that is lost or that you'll never have."

As we get older, we also give ourselves credit for having learned something along the way. In a study of men and women in their fifties, reported in *Gerontologist*, sociologist David Karp, Ph.D., found that people felt good about being this age; one word that came up frequently was "wisdom." His subjects saw their lives from a larger point of view. Joanne puts it this way: "I like having all the experience, the perspective that comes out of fifty-five or sixty years, having a sense of the historical passage of time and my place in it. It's anchoring. I like being able to start myself from the time of World War

II. I'm thankful that I experienced all that I did during that time; I feel enriched by it."

But accepting ourselves doesn't mean that it's time to stop changing. Researchers in successful aging have found that among other things, two factors are most vital: First, we need a purpose in life, a sense of directedness, and goals that give us meaning. And second, we need to feel that we are continuing to grow and reaching our potential. Part of aging in a good way is, as Sarah puts it, "growth and openness and the ability to keep learning. To be able to always start again, that's the secret."

In our fifties, we still have the desire and the power to create our own narratives, and we're nowhere near ready to write the last act. Says Marlene, "My mentor was Maggie Kuhn, who started the Gray Panthers at seventy. Whenever I think I'm not doing anything big enough, I say, 'Well, I've got twenty more years before I even have to get started.'"

One of the most inspiring things about interviewing the women for this book was hearing how they see themselves in the future. Some of us have amazingly ambitious goals. Joanne was only half joking when she enumerated this list: "I'd like to have more energy, a more incisive mind; to memorize the nations of Africa and a long poem; to be good at crossword puzzles; to be able to dance all night and not get tired, to eat half a pie and not gain weight, to have sex three times a week and be multiorgasmic (but within a half hour so as not to spend too much time), and to feel fabulous afterward and have that kind of closeness where you start weeping; to be a good artist; to express myself creatively, to draw or paint; to write poetry; to have more time for my children; to understand the computer more; to travel and learn a new language; to make necklaces for friends; to have more time for sewing." Then she got serious: "I'd like to do something that really makes a difference in people's lives. I'm afraid of dying with regrets that I could have been of more use."

The fundamental nature of life is growth and change. During our fifties we have an opportunity to stop the tapes that have been running since childhood and come up with a new definition of ourselves. For some of us, a clear, stunning moment starts the voyage. My husband's betrayal and our divorce triggered my ongoing transformation from supporting player to star of my own show; this book is the evidence. For other women, the process is more gradual. But either way, the stories of fifty-something women are stories of women in transition.

One year after my husband left, I threw myself a combination birthday/I've-made-it-through-the-first-year party. As we ate dinner, drank wine, and talked into the night, it was striking to hear how—from careers to twenty-something children to menopause to aging parents to changing marriages to the different ways that men and women face mortality and think about happiness—we fifty-something women are putting all aspects of our lives on the table. There are no established rites of passage to mark our journey. Instead, as we stand poised on the threshold to the next act of our lives, we learn from each other how to reclaim or reinvent our best and truest selves.

BIBLIOGRAPHY

INTRODUCTION

Sexton, L. "Between Two Worlds." *Radcliffe Quarterly* 66(1) (1980): 5–8.

Apter, Terri. *Secret Paths: Women in the New Midlife.* New York: W. W. Norton and Company, 1995.

Bart, Pauline. "Depression in Middle-Aged Women." In *Women in a Sexist Society*, edited by Vivian Gornick and Barbara Moran. New York: BasicBooks, 1971.

CHAPTER 1

Berg, Elizabeth. *The Pull of the Moon.* New York: Random House, 1996.

Bolen, Jean Shinoda. *Goddesses in Older Women.* New York: HarperCollins, 2001.

Brett, Belle. "The Radcliffe Class of 1969: Women on the Cutting Edge." In *Women's Lives Through Time*, edited by Kathleen Day Hulbert and Diane Tickton Schuster. San Francisco: Jossey-Bass Publishers, 1993.

Edelstein, Linda N. *The Art of Midlife.* Westport: Bergin & Garvey, 1999.

Gould, Roger. *Transformations: Growth and Change in Adult Life.* New York: Simon and Schuster, 1978.

Dreifus, Claudia. "Ms. Behavin' Again." *Modern Maturity*, May/June 1999.

Josselson, Ruthellen. *Revising Herself.* New York: Oxford University Press, 1996.

Carter, Bill. "After 27 Years, Pauley Plans to Leave NBC in May." *New York Times*, February 20, 2003.

CHAPTER 2

Jong, Erica. *Fear of Fifty.* New York: Harper Paperbacks, 1994.

Hollis, James. *The Middle Passage.* Toronto: Inner City Books, 1993.

Jordan, Judith V. "The Meaning of Mutuality." In *Women's Growth in Connection*, by Judith Jordan et al. New York: The Guilford Press, 1991.

Spraggins, Renee E. *Women in the United States: A Profile.* Current Population Reports, CENBR/00–1, U.S. Census Bureau: Washington, D.C., 2000.

Baruch, Grace, Rosalind Barnett, and Caryl Rivers. *Lifeprints: New Patterns of Love & Work for Today's Women.* New York: Plume, 1984.

Fields, Jason, and Lynne M. Casper. *America's Families and Living Arrangements: March 2000.* Current Population Reports, P20–537, U.S. Census Bureau: Washington, D.C., 2001.

Bart, Pauline. "The Paradox of the Happy Marriage." In *Women in a Sexist Society*, edited by Vivian Gornick and Barbara Moran. New York: Basic Books, 1971.

Neugarten, Bernice L. "The Awareness of Middle Age." In *Middle Age and Aging.* Chicago: The University of Chicago Press, 1968.

Gilbert, Susan. "New Portrait of Retiring Is Emerging." *New York Times*, May 29, 2001.

Friedman, Ariella. "Getting Powerful with Age: Changes in Women over the Life Cycle." *Israel Social Science Research* 5, no. 1–2 (1987): 76–86.

Masters, William H., and Virginia E. Johnson. "Human Sexual Response: The Aging Female and the Aging Male." In *Middle Age and Aging*, edited by Bernice L. Neugarten. Chicago: The University of Chicago Press, 1968.

Rubin, Lillian B. *Women of a Certain Age.* New York: Harper & Row, 1979.

Northrup, Christiane. *The Wisdom of Menopause.* New York: Bantam Books, 2001.

Stiver, Irene P. "The Meanings of 'Dependency' in Female–Male Relationships." In *Women's Growth in Connection*, by Judith Jordan et al. New York: The Guilford Press, 1991.

Dennerstein, L., A. M. A. Smith, C. A. Morse, and H. Burger. "Sexuality and the Menopause," *Journal of Psychosomatic Obstetrics and Gynaecology* 15 (1994): 59–66.

Ruben, Harvey. *Supermarriage: Overcoming the Predictable Crises of Married Life.* New York: Bantam Books, 1986.

Updike, John. "The Red-Herring Theory." In *Too Far To Go: The Maples Stories*. New York: Fawcett Crest Books, 1979.

Taylor, Shelley E. *The Tending Instinct*. New York: Times Books, 2002.

Kiecolt-Glaser, J. K., and T. L. Newton. "Marriage and Health: His and Hers." *Psychological Bulletin*. 127, no. 4(2001): 472–503.

CHAPTER 3

Watkins, S .C., J. A. Menken, and J. Bongaarts. "Demographic Foundations of Family Change." *American Sociological Review* 52 (1987): 346–358.

Popenoe, David. "The Top Ten Myths of Divorce" The National Marriage Project at Rutgers University, May 2001.

Holmes & Rahe. "Holmes-Rahe Life Changes Scale." *Journal of Psychosomatic Research* 11 (1967): 213–218.

Kreider, Rose M., and Jason Fields. "Number, Timing and Duration of Marriages and Divorces: 1996," U.S. Census Bureau: Current Population Reports (February 2002): 70–80.

Uchitelle, Louis, "Lacking Pensions, Older Divorced Women Remain at Work." *New York Times*, June 26, 2001.

Dubus, Andre. "The Winter Father." In *Fault Lines: Stories of Divorce*, edited by Caitlin Shetterly. New York: Berkley Books, 2001.

"A Working Woman's Guide to Financial Security," Published by University of Illinois Cooperative Extension Service, www.urbanext. uiuc.edu/ww1.

Miller, Jean Baker. *Toward a New Psychology of Women*. Boston: Beacon Press, 1986.

Buchan, Elizabeth. *The Revenge of the Middle-Aged Woman*. New York: Viking, 2003.

Taylor, Shelley E. *The Tending Instinct*. New York: Times Books, 2002.

Hayes, Christopher, Deborah Anderson, and Melinda Blau. *Our Turn: Women Who Triumph in the Face of Divorce*. New York: Pocket Books, 1993.

Personal communication with Trish McDermott and Bridgette Cush at Match.com, November 2002.

Gebhard, Paul. "Postmarital Coitus Among Widows and Divorcees." In *Divorce and After*, edited by Paul Bohannan. Garden City, New York: Anchor Books, 1971.

Census Bureau *Facts for Features*. Valentine's Day: February 14. CB98–FS.02, January 29, 1998.

CHAPTER 4

"Donor-Egg Pregnancies Called Safe After Age 50." *New York Times*, November 13, 2002.

Mathews, T. J., and B. E. Hamilton. Mean age of mother, 1970–2000. National Vital Statistics Reports 51, no. 1. Hyattsville, Maryland: National Center for Health Statistics, 2002.

Brett, Belle. "The Radcliffe Class of 1969: Women on the Cutting Edge." In *Women's Lives Through Time*, edited by Kathleen Day Hulbert and Diane Tickton Schuster. San Francisco: Jossey-Bass Publishers, 1993.

Glenn, N. "Psychological Well-Being in the Postparental Stage: Some Evidence from National Surveys." *Journal of Marriage and the Family* 37 (1975): 105–110.

Bachu, Amara, and Martin O'Connell. *Fertility of American Women: June 2000*. Current Population Reports, P20–543RV. U.S. Census Bureau: Washington, D.C., 2001.

Gutmann, David. *Reclaimed Powers*. Evanston, Illinois: Northwestern University Press, 1994.

Baruch, Grace, Rosalind Barnett, and Caryl Rivers. *Lifeprints: New Patterns of Love & Work for Today's Women*. New York: Plume, 1984.

"FactSheet: Gay, Lesbian and Bisexual Issues." American Psychiatric Association, May 2000, www.psych.org/public_info.

Miller, Jean Baker. *Toward a New Psychology of Women*. Boston: Beacon Press, 1986.

Gilligan, C. *In a Different Voice*. Cambridge, Massachusetts: Harvard University Press, 1982.

Silverberg, Susan S. "Parents' Well-Being at Their Children's Transition to Adolescence." In *The Parental Experience in Midlife*, edited by Carol D. Ryff and Marsha Mailick Seltzer. Chicago: The University of Chicago Press, 1996.

Rubin, Lillian B. *Women of a Certain Age*. New York: Harper & Row, 1979.

Umberson, D., and Gove, W. R. "Parenthood and Psychological Well-Being: Theory, Measurement, and Stage in the Family Life Course." *Journal of Family Issues* 10 (1989): 440-462.

Crittenden, Ann. *The Price of Motherhood*. New York: Metropolitan Books, 2001.

Seltzer, Marsha Mailick, and Carol D. Ryff. "The Parental Experience in Midlife: Past, Present and Future." In *The Parental Experience in Midlife*. Chicago: The University of Chicago Press, 1996.

Friday, Nancy. *My Mother/My Self*. New York: Delacorte Press, 1977.

Graber, Julia A., and Jeanne Brooks-Gunn. "Reproductive Transitions: The Experience of Mothers and Daughters." In *The Parental Experience in Midlife*, edited by Carol D. Ryff and Marsha Mailick Seltzer. Chicago: The University of Chicago Press, 1996.

La Sorsa, V. A., and I. G. Fodor. "Adolescent Daughter/Midlife Mother Dyad: A New Look at Separation and Self-Definition." *Psychology of Women Quarterly* 14 (1990): 593–606.

CHAPTER 5

Carter, Betty, and Joan K. Peters. *Love, Honor and Negotiate*. New York: Pocket Books, 1996.

Thurnher, Majda, David Chiriboga, Marjorie Fisk Lowenthal, et. al. *Four Stages of Life: A Comparative Study of Men and Women Facing Transitions*. San Francisco: Jossey-Bass Publishers, 1975.

George, Linda K., and Deborah T. Gold. "Life Course Perspectives on Intergenerational and Generational Connections." *Marriage and Family Review* 6 (1991): 67–88.

Deutscher, Irwin. "The Quality of Postparental Life." In *Middle Age and Aging*, edited by Bernice L. Neugarten. Chicago: The University of Chicago Press, 1968.

Greider, Linda. "Hard Times Drive Adult Kids 'Home.'" *AARP Bulletin*, December 2001.

Aquilino, W. S. "The Likelihood of Parent-Adult Child Coresidence: Effects of Family Structure and Parental Characteristics." *Journal of Marriage and the Family* 52 (1990): 405–419.

DaVanzo, Julie, and Frances K. Goldscheider. "Coming Home Again: Returns to the Parental Home of Young Adults." *Population Studies* 44, no. 2 (1990): 241–55.

Bramlett, M. D., and W. D. Mosher. "Cohabitation, Marriage, Divorce, and Remarriage in the United States." National Center for Health Statistics. Vital Health Stat 23, no. 22, 2002.

"New Report Sheds Light on Trends and Patterns in Marriage, Divorce and Cohabitation." National Center for Health Statistics Fact Sheet, July 24, 2002. [The average age for a first marriage is 27 for men and 25 for women.]

Fields, Jason, and Lynne M. Casper. *America's Families and Living Arrangements: March 2000.* Current Population Reports, P20–537. U.S. Census Bureau: Washington, D.C., 2001.

Lewin, Tamar. "Parents' Role Is Narrowing Generation Gap on Campus." *New York Times*, January 6, 2003.

CHAPTER 6

Nemy, Enid. "Mary Kay Ash, Builder of Beauty Empire, Dies at 83." *New York Times*, November 14, 2001.

Schuster, Diane Tickton. "Studying Women's Lives Through Time." In *Women's Lives Through Time*, edited by Kathleen Day Hulbert and Diane Tickton Schuster. San Francisco: Jossey-Bass Publishers, 1993.

Giele, Janet Zollinger. "Women's Role Change and Adaptation, 1920–1990." In *Women's Lives Through Time*, edited by Kathleen Day Hulbert and Diane Tickton Schuster. San Francisco: Jossey-Bass Publishers, 1993.

Spraggins, Renee E. *Women in the United States: A Profile.* Current Population Reports, CENBR/00–1, U.S. Census Bureau: Washington, D.C., 2000.

Morris, Betsy. "Is Your Family Wrecking Your Career?" *Fortune*, March 17, 1997, 70.

Brett, Belle. "The Radcliffe Class of 1969: Women on the Cutting Edge," in *Women's Lives Through Time*, edited by Kathleen Day Hulbert and Diane Tickton Schuster (San Francisco: Jossey-Bass Publishers, 1993).

Inglehart, Marita, Donald R. Brown, and Oksana Malanchuk. "University of Michigan Medical School Graduates of the 1980s: The Professional

Development of Women Physicians." In *Women's Lives Through Time*, edited by Kathleen Day Hulbert and Diane Tickton Schuster. San Francisco: Jossey-Bass Publishers, 1993.

McIntosh, Peggy. "Feeling Like a Fraud." Stone Center for Developmental Services and Studies, Wellesley Centers for Women, 1985.

Berg, Elizabeth. *The Pull of the Moon*. New York: Random House, 1996.

Hinden, Stan. "Raw Deal for Women?" *AARP Bulletin*, September 2001.

Leonhardt, David. "Wage Gap Between Men and Women Is Narrowest Ever." *New York Times*, February 17, 2003.

Glasheen, Leah K., and Susan L. Crowley. "More Women in Driver's Seat." *AARP Bulletin*, November 1999.

Waldfogel, Jane. "Understanding the 'Family Gap' in Pay for Women with Children." *The Journal of Economic Perspectives* 12, no. 1 (Winter 1998): 137–56.

"Women and the MBA: Gateway to Opportunity." 2000 Catalyst, Center for the Education of Women at the University of Michigan, and University of Michigan Business School.

Reis, Sally Morgan. *Work Left Undone*. Mansfield Center, Connecticut: Creative Learning Press, Inc., 1998.

Nicholson, Trish. "Boomers Discover Age Bias." *AARP Bulletin*, March 2003.

Executive Summary. "Good for Business: Making Full Use of the Nation's Human Capital." *The Environmental Scan*, issued March 1995, Washington, D.C.

"As Leaders, Women Rule." *Business Week*, November 20, 2000, 74.

Trottman, Melanie. "After Work Comes . . . More Work." *The Wall Street Journal*, November 29, 1999.

Uchitelle, Louis. "Lacking Pensions, Older Divorced Women Remain at Work." *New York Times*, June 26, 2001.

Shaw, Lois, and Catherine Hill. "The Gender Gap in Pension Coverage: What Does the Future Hold?" The Institute for Women's Policy Research, 2002.

Fields, Jason, and Lynne M. Casper. *America's Families and Living Arrangements: March 2000*. Current Population Reports, P20–537, U.S. Census Bureau: Washington, D.C., 2001.

CHAPTER 7

Kaufert, Patricia A., and Margaret Lock. "What Are Women For?" In *In Her Prime: New Views of Middle-Aged Women*, edited by Virginia Kerns and Judith K. Brown. University of Illinois Press, 1992.

Reuben, David. *Everything You Always Wanted to Know about Sex But Were Afraid to Ask*. New York: David McKay Company, Inc., 1969.

Wilson, Robert A. *Feminine Forever*. New York: Pocket Books, 1968.

Neugarten, Bernice, et al. "Women's Attitudes Toward the Menopause." In *Middle Age and Aging*, edited by Bernice L. Neugarten. Chicago: The University of Chicago Press, 1968.

McKinlay, J. B., S. M. McKinlay, and D J. Brambilla. "The Relative Contributions of Endocrine Changes and Social Circumstances to Depression in Mid-Aged Women." *Journal of Health and Social Behavior* 28, no. 4 (1987): 345–63.

Menopause Core Curriculum Study Guide, Section A. The North American Menopause Society, October 2002. www.menopause.org/aboutmeno/overview.html.

"Life Expectancy By Age, Race and Sex." National Vital Statistics Reports 51, no. 3, December 19, 2002.

Northrup, Christiane. *The Wisdom of Menopause*. New York: Bantam Books, 2001.

Shields, Carol. *Happenstance*. New York: Penguin Books, 1994.

Strickland, B.R. "Women and Depression." *Current Directions in Psychological Science* 1 (1992): 132–35.

"Taking Charge of 'The Change': Dealing with the Downside of Menopause," in *Facts of Life* 8, no. 1, January 2003. Center for the Advancement of Health, Washington, D.C.

Kaufert, Patricia, et al. "Women and Menopause: Beliefs, Attitudes, and Behaviors. The North American Menopause Society 1997 Menopause Survey." *Menopause: The Journal of The North American Menopause Society* 5, no. 4 (1998): 197–202.

Tallmer, Margot. "The Mid-Life Crisis in Women." In *Women and Loss*. New York: Praeger Publishers, 1985, 22–29.

Cunningham, Michael. *The Hours*. New York: Picador USA, 2002.

Rossi, Alice S., and Peter H. Rossi. *Of Human Bonding*. New York: Aldine de Gruyter, 1990.

Acocella, Joan. "Out of Character." *The New Yorker*, March 3, 2003.

"Percent of Change in Selected Procedures: 1997–2001." The American Society for Aesthetic Plastic Surgery, www.surgery.org/press/2001-percentchange.asp.

La Ferla, Ruth. "Middle-Aged Lovers Jostle Onto the Screen." *New York Times*, January 13, 2002.

Dorothy Sayers quote from Heilbrun, Carolyn G. *Writing a Woman's Life*. New York: Ballantine Books.

Rubenstein, Carin. "All Shook Up." *My Generation*, March–April 2001, 20–25.

Lark, Susan. "Women's Health Update from Susan Lark, M.D." *Empowering Women, Restoring Health*, September 17, 2003.

CHAPTER 8

Livesey, Margot. "The Valley of Lost Things." In *Between Friends*, edited by Mickey Pearlman. New York: Houghton Mifflin Company, 1994.

Gilligan, C. *In a Different Voice*. Cambridge, Massachusetts: Harvard University Press, 1982.

Miller, Jean Baker. *Toward a New Psychology of Women*. Boston: Beacon Press, 1986.

Borysenko, Joan. *A Woman's Journey to God*. New York: Riverhead Books, 1999.

Rubin, Lillian. *Just Friends*. New York: Harper & Row, 1985.

Vera Brittain quote from Heilbrun, Carolyn G. *Writing a Woman's Life*. New York: Ballantine Books.

Smiley, Jane. "Can Writers Have Friends?" In *Between Friends*, edited by Mickey Pearlman. New York: Houghton Mifflin Company, 1994.

Munro, Alice. "What Is Remembered." In *Hateship, Friendship, Courtship, Love and Marriage: Stories*. New York: Knopf, 2001.

Taylor, S. E., L. C. Klein, B. P. Lewis, T. L. Gruenewald, R. A. R. Gurung, and J. A. Updegraff. "Female Responses to Stress: Tend-and-Befriend, Not Fight-or-Flight." *Psychological Review*, 107, no. 3 (2000): 411–29.

Older Women. Fact Sheet from the U.S. Agency on Aging, Washington, D.C., May 2000.

Vaillant, George. *Aging Well.* New York: Little Brown & Company, 2002.

Berg, Elizabeth. *The Pull of the Moon.* New York: Random House, 1996.

CHAPTER 9

Hagestad, Gunhild O. "Demographic Change and the Life Course: Some Emerging Trends in the Family Realm." *Family Relations* 37, no. 4 (October 1988): 405–10.

Pipher, Mary. *Another Country.* New York: Riverhead Books, 1999.

Erikson, Erik H. *Childhood and Society.* New York: W. W. Norton and Company, 1950.

Butler, R. N. "The Life Review: An Interpretation of Reminiscence in the Aged." *Psychiatry* 26 (1963): 65–76.

Umberson, Debra. "Relationships Between Adult Children and Their Parents: Psychological Consequences for Both Generations." *Journal of Marriage and the Family* 54 (1992): 664–74.

Franzen, Jonathan. *The Corrections.* New York: Farrar, Straus and Giroux, 2001.

Josselson, Ruthellen. *Revising Herself.* New York: Oxford University Press, 1996.

Brett, Belle. "The Radcliffe Class of 1969: Women on the Cutting Edge." In *Women's Lives Through Time,* edited by Kathleen Day Hulbert and Diane Tickton Schuster. San Francisco: Jossey-Bass Publishers, 1993.

Friday, Nancy. *My Mother/My Self.* New York: Delacorte Press, 1977.

Edelman, Hope. *Motherless Daughters.* New York: Delta, 1994.

Family Caregiving in the U.S.. The National Alliance for Caregiving, Bethesda, MD, and the American Association of Retired Persons: Washington, D.C., June 1997.

Merrill, Deborah. *Caring for Elderly Parents.* Westport, CT: Auburn House, 1997.

Garland, Susan B. "Faraway Relatives Turning to Geriatrics Experts." *New York Times,* January 19, 2003.

The MetLife Juggling Act Study. Metropolitan Life Insurance Company: New York, 1999.

Hollis, James. *The Middle Passage.* Toronto: Inner City Books, 1993.

CHAPTER 10

Neugarten, Bernice. "Time, Age and the Life Cycle." *American Journal of Psychiatry* 136, no. 7 (1979): 887–94.

Rubenstein, Carin. "All Shook Up." *My Generation.* March–April 2001, 20–25.

Winter, Miriam Therese, Adair T. Lummis, and Allison Stokes. *Defecting in Place.* New York: Crossroad Publishing Company, 1994.

Roof, Wade Clark. *A Generation of Seekers.* HarperSanFrancisco, 1993.

Johnson, Sally. "Getting Down and Dirty in the Garden is Big Business." *New York Times*, September 28, 1996.

"Who's Who Among Today's Gardeners." The National Gardening Association, National Gardening Survey 2001, www.garden.org/RSRCH/feature_july.asp.

Ogden, Gina. *Sexuality and Spirituality in Women's Relationships* (Wellesley Centers for Women Working Paper No. 405). Wellesley, Massachusetts: Wellesley Centers for Women, 2002.

Campbell, Joseph. *The Power of Myth.* New York: Doubleday, 1988.

Erikson, Erik H. *Childhood and Society.* New York: W. W. Norton and Company, 1950.

"Who Volunteers?" *AARP Bulletin*, December 2001.

AFTERWORD

Aldwin, Carolyn M., Karen J. Sutton, and Margie Lachman. "The Development of Coping Resources in Adulthood." *Journal of Personality* 64, no. 4 (December 1996): 837–71.

Moen, Phyllis, Donna Moen Dempster-McClain, and Robin M. Williams Jr. "Social Integration and Longevity: An Event History Analysis of Women's Roles and Resilience." *American Sociological Review* 54 (August 1989): 635–47.

Moen, Phyllis, Donna Moen Dempster-McClain, and Robin M. Williams Jr. "Successful Aging: A Life-Course Perspective on Women's Multiple Roles and Health." *American Journal of Sociology* 97, no. 6 (May 1992): 1612–38.

Belenky, Mary Field, et al. *Women's Ways of Knowing*. New York: BasicBooks, Inc., 1997.

Giele, Janet Zollinger. "Women's Role Change and Adaptation, 1920–1990." In *Women's Lives Through Time*, edited by Kathleen Day Hulbert and Diane Tickton Schuster. San Francisco: Jossey-Bass Publishers, 1993.

Markus, Hazel, and Paula Nurius. "Possible Selves." *American Psychologist* 41, no. 9 (September 1986): 954–68.

Jordan, Judith. "Relational Resilience." Stone Center for Developmental Services and Studies, Wellesley Centers for Women, 1992.

Graham, Katharine. *Personal History*. New York: Alfred A. Knopf, Inc., 1997.

Karp, David A. "A Decade of Reminders: Changing Age Consciousness Between Fifty and Sixty Years Old." *Gerontologist* 18, no. 6 (December 1988): 727–38.